KEYSTONES OF THE WORLD

KEYSTONES OF THE WORLD

Ten Narratives Highlighting

the Significance of Stones in the Torah

Devorah Reich

TARGUM/FELDHEIM

First published 2002
Copyright © 2002 by Devorah Reich
ISBN 1-56871-220-0

All rights reserved

No part of this publication may be translated, reproduced, stored
in a retrieval system, or transmitted in any form or by any means,
electronic, mechanical, photocopying, recording, or otherwise,
without prior permission in writing from both the copyright
holder and the publisher.

Published by:
TARGUM PRESS, INC.
22700 W. Eleven Mile Rd.
Southfield, MI 48034
E-mail: targum@netvision.net.il
Fax: 888-298-9992
www.targum.com

Distributed by:
FELDHEIM PUBLISHERS
202 Airport Executive Park
Nanuet, NY 10954

Printed in Israel

RABBI. O.Y. WESTHEIM
Dayan, Manchester Beis Din
Rav of Beis Hamedrash Zeirei Agudas Yisroel

אשר יעקב וועסטהײם
דומו״צ בבד״יץ דק״ק מאנשעסטער
רב דביהמ״ד צא״י בק״ק חנ״יל

15, Broom Lane,
Salford M7 4EQ
Tel: 0161 792 4939
Fax: 0161 792 5124

בס״יד

י״א טבת ד׳ לסדר ״ומשם רועה אבן ישראלי״, היתשנ״יט לבח״יע
30th December '98

This book is a testimony to the vast knowledge of its author, Miss D. Reich.
She has succesfully shown the significance of stones throughout Tenach in
Torah terms. Her work illuminates many Pesukim and Parshiyos which are
not always fully appreciated. She has also very ably synchronised Divrei
Chazal with the words of Tenach - which has all helped to create a delightful
Sefer which will be a treasured addition to any Jewish bookshelf.

Perhaps the most important reference to stones is that in Parshas Vayechi
(48-24) - משם רועה **אבן** ישראל, which refers to the unity of Klal Yisroel (see
Ha'amek Dovor), and in particular to the bond between parents and children.
The word **אבן** alludes to the two words אב ובן - father and son (see Rashi).
The strong bond between them is the cornerstone of the survival of Klal
Yisroel.

This concept may give even greater depth to this excellent publication.

I wish the authoress much success.

Contents

Acknowledgments 9

Introduction 11

One: The Foundation Stone of the World 13

Two: Yaakov's Pillar 26

Three: The Stone on the Mouth of the Well . . . 35

Four: The Stone of Israel 48

Five: The Tablets 54

Six: The Rock of Kadesh 77

Seven: The Inscription on the Stones 105

Eight: David Vanquishes Golias 140

Nine: The Altar 164

Ten: The Temple 178

Glossary 193

Sources 197

Acknowledgments

Firstly, I would like to thank my father for his help and encouragement. His unfailing erudition was an inspiration. I am grateful too for my mother's constructive suggestions and express warm thanks to my brothers Shloime and Shaul for their support and assistance respectively.

I am indebted to Dayan ʿOsher Westheim for his *haskamah* and to Rabbi Nosson Dovid Rabinowich for his valuable comments. I would also like to thank Rabbi Dov Sternbuch for allowing me to use his *divrei Torah*.

Finally, many thanks to the staff at Targum Press — Rabbi Moshe Dombey, editors Miriam Zakon and Suri Brand, and graphic artist D. Liff.

Introduction

Stone. Inanimate stone. At a superficial level, what could be more ordinary and prosaic? But this ubiquitous element has played a surprisingly major role in the history and development of our people.

Well before the birth of the Jewish nation, this material was no less than vital, for the earth itself was established with the *even shesiyah*, the foundation stone of the world.

Two thousand years later our forefather Yaakov came upon this same foundation stone. And it was he who effortlessly rolled a huge stone from the mouth of the well in an episode rich with portents for the future. Moreover, in his blessing to Yosef, Yaakov refers to the "stone of Israel," which some interpret as an allusion to the nation of Israel. But the Jewish people only acquired their unique identity when they received the Ten Commandments, which of course were inscribed on tablets of stone.

Not every association with stone is pleasant, however. In one of the most painful and dramatic incidents recorded in the Torah, Moshe struck the rock and was consequently denied entry into the Land of Israel. But Moshe, too, instructed the people to write the entire Torah upon large stones, and this multifaceted command-ment was carried out in the time of Yehoshua.

What was the weapon that felled the mighty Golias? None other than a stone thrown by King David. David also built the altar that was later to become a part of the Temple. This altar and its successor in the Second Temple were made of stone, whereas the Tabernacle housed a copper altar.

❖　❖　❖

The aim of this book is to explore these significant episodes in our history and heritage. In this context, no words are more apposite than those written by King Shlomo in *Koheles*: "For everything there is a season and a time for every purpose under the heavens...*a time to gather stones together*" (*Koheles* 3:1, 5).

Chapter One
The Foundation Stone of the World

Formed from fire, air, and water, the *even shesiyah* is the kernel of creation. During the era of the Temple, it stood within the Holy of Holies, on the most sacred site in the entire world. Not far from the *even shesiyah*, in the area of the Temple Mount, the *akeidah*, the binding of Yitzchak, was enacted. (The famous rock on the Temple Mount today is probably the *even shesiyah* — see photograph on page 14.)

A *mishnah* in the Talmud describes the *even shesiyah*:

> From the time when the *Aron* was taken [i.e., at the end of the era of the first Temple], a stone was there from the days of the early prophets, and it was called *shesiyah*; [it was] three fingers above the ground, and on it [the *kohen gadol*] would put [the firepan containing the incense].
>
> (*Yoma* 5:2)

The early prophets referred to in the *mishnah* are Shmuel and King David; it was in their time that the stone was revealed. The *mishnah* then states that the *kohen gadol* would put the firepan on the *even shesiyah*.

During the period of the first Temple, the *Aron*, the Holy Ark, rested on the *even shesiyah* in the Holy of

Holies. In the course of the Yom Kippur service, the *kohen gadol* would place the firepan of incense between the two poles of the Ark and burn the incense there. But with the destruction of the first Temple, the *Aron* was no longer present; it was either exiled or completely buried. So when the Temple was rebuilt, where did the *kohen gadol* put the firepan? It was placed on the *even shesiyah*, next to where the Ark had formerly rested. Immediately after placing the firepan on the stone, the *kohen gadol* would leave the Holy of Holies and pray for the welfare of the Jewish people for the coming year.

The Midrash quotes a verse from the book of *Iyov* that depicts the response of the Shechinah, the Divine Pres-

The ancient rock on the Temple Mount, thought to be the *even shesiyah*.

ence, to the loss of the *Aron*: סלע ישכון ויתלונן על שן סלע ומצודה, "It dwells on the rock, and it lodges upon the crag of the rock and the fortress" (*Iyov* 39:28). "It *dwells* on the rock" refers to the era of the first Beis HaMikdash. Then the Shechinah rested serenely on the rock — the *Aron* — which was a fitting residence for the Divine Presence.

The second Beis HaMikdash was bereft of the Ark, but the *even shesiyah* remained. That became the resting place of the Shechinah, but with a vast difference: "It *lodges* upon the crag of the rock and the fortress." In this part of the verse, the Shechinah is compared to a reluctant guest forced to make do with the lodgings that are available. The *even shesiyah*, which protruded from the ground like the sharp point of a rock, was not the Shechinah's real home; it was regarded merely as a temporary accommodation. But the stone was, nevertheless, the foundation of the world. For this reason it is compared to a fortress, which is synonymous with strength.

The Title

Why was this stone called the אבן שתיה, the foundation stone? The Talmud explains, ממנה הושתת העולם, "The world was founded from it."

A *midrash* helps to clarify this concept. Just as the navel is in the center of the body, so the Land of Israel is situated in the center of the world. Jerusalem is in the middle of the Land of Israel, the Temple in the middle of Jerusalem, the Inner Chamber in the middle of the Temple, and the Ark in the middle of the Inner Chamber. The *even shesiyah* is underneath the Ark, and this stone was

16   *Keystones of the World*

the starting point for the creation of the earth.

God built the world around the *even shesiyah* and Jerusalem; He began from what would be the innermost point and worked His way outward. We find an allusion to this in *Tehillim*: "A psalm of Asaf: God, God, Hashem, has spoken and called the earth, from the rising of the sun to its setting. From Zion, the perfection of beauty, God has shone forth" (*Tehillim* 50:1–2). A verse from Iyov gives us a further insight into God's methods of creation: "When the dust runs into a mass and the clods cleave fast together" (*Iyov* 38:38). First Zion — the "mass" — was created. This block of solid matter was then surrounded with clods of earth. Thus the structure grew and grew until the world was complete.

A parallel thought is found in another Midrashic source, in the form of an analogy. Man is considered a small world; thus the formation of a human being corresponds to the creation of the world. Just as an embryo starts to grow from its navel and spreads forth in every direction, so the world began with the *even shesiyah* and continued to develop outward.

In an entirely different vein, one commentator states that the purpose of the earth was *fixed and established* in the place of the *even shesiyah* — hence its name. God's intentions for the world became apparent on this site.

Another commentator bases his interpretation on the *mishnah* "The world rests on three things: on Torah study, on the service of God, and on kind deeds" (*Avos* 1:2). "Service of God" refers to the sacrificial offerings in the Temple. The *even shesiyah*, central to the Temple, is so named because the sacrifices are one of the foundations of the world.

Yaakov, Yonah, and the *Even Shesiyah*

Our forefather Yaakov slept on the site of the *even shesiyah*, and it was there that he dreamed his wondrous dream. The next morning he exclaimed, "How awesome is this place! This is none other than the House of God, and this is the gate of Heaven" (*Bereishis* 28:17).

A commentator on the Midrash explains that the place of the *even shesiyah* is of vital importance. All of God's bounty and blessing, all the lifegiving material that sustains the entire planet, descend first to that particular spot.

The heart is king of all the organs in the body; it is this central powerhouse that first receives energy from the food we eat, before pumping life and strength to every vein and limb. Likewise, the site of the *even shesiyah* is the center of the earth, receiving every form of goodness needed by man. This cornucopia is then distributed to all the inhabitants of the world. This is why Yaakov called the place of the *even shesiyah* "the gate of Heaven" — it is the first gate for receiving the Heavenly blessings.

Moreover, it is here that "the land and the sky kiss" (*Bava Basra* 74a). All the prayers we utter, whether they are words of thanks, praise, or supplication, ascend to Heaven from that spot. And in response, the blessings of God descend first to the site of the *even shesiyah*.

But there is a deeper connection between Yaakov and the *even shesiyah*, one that had an impact on the entire cosmos. The Midrash vividly describes what happened.

On that night God showed Yaakov many signs. He showed him a ladder stretching from the ground until the heavens. Angels were ascending and descending the ladder, and when they saw Yaakov, they said, "This face is like the face of the *Chayah* [a category of angel], which is on the Throne of Glory!"

Yaakov rose early in a state of great fear and said, "This is none other than the House of God, and this is the gate of Heaven" (*Bereishis* 28:17). We learn from this that praying at that site in Jerusalem is equivalent to praying before the Throne of Glory. "The gate of Heaven" is an open door for prayer.

The evening before, Yaakov had placed a number of stones around his head as a protection during his sleep (in chapter 2 this topic is discussed in detail). Now he went to gather the stones, but he discovered that they had merged and become one! Yaakov set up this stone as a pillar.

Oil miraculously descended from Heaven, and he poured it on the pillar. Then God "stretched out His right foot" and sank the pillar into the uttermost depths of the earth. The stone became a keystone for the world, analogous to the insertion of a keystone into an arch (it holds the structure together). The *even shesiyah* served the purpose of strengthening and supporting the world.

It is called the *even shesiyah*, the foundation stone, because it is from there that the world began, and that same stone enabled the world to continue. Upon it stood God's Temple, as Yaakov said, "And this stone that I have

The Foundation Stone of the World 19

set up as a pillar shall be the House of God" (*Bereishis* 28:22).

Yaakov fell on his face before the *even shesiyah* and prayed to God. He said, "Master of the universe! If You return me safely to this place, I will sacrifice thanksgiving offerings and burnt offerings before You," as it is written, "And Yaakov vowed a vow..." (ibid., 20).

One commentator gives another reason for the name of this stone. When Yaakov poured oil on the pillar, the stone drank the oil, so to speak, and therefore it is described as the *even shesiyah*. (The word *shesiyah* can be translated as "drinking" rather than "foundation.")

The *midrash* also explains how Yonah came upon the *even shesiyah*.

Yonah, while inside the fish, was shown wonderful sights that were in the ocean and the depths of the world, among these the *even shesiyah* at the base of the Temple. He saw the sons of Korach standing on the stone and praying. This place had been reserved for them from ancient times, and here they stood, prayed, and sang praises to their Creator.

The fish said to Yonah, "You are standing underneath God's Temple! Pray and you will be answered." Yonah prayed, and the fish cast him out onto dry land.

The Wisdom of King Shlomo

King Shlomo also refers to the *even shesiyah*, although more indirectly than Yaakov.

In *Shir HaShirim* Shlomo describes the world God created.

Keystones of the World

> King Shlomo made an *apiryon* for himself from the wood of Lebanon. He made its pillars of silver, its hangings were gold, its seat purple, its inner side was decked with love by the daughters of Jerusalem.
>
> *(Shir HaShirim 3:9–10)*

There are various Midrashic interpretations of the word *apiryon*. One meaning is the "world." And of course it was not a human king who created the world, but God Himself. Thus Shlomo was referring to God when he wrote, "King Shlomo made an *apiryon*"; שלמה implies שהשלום שלו, "He to Whom peace belongs." The material He used was the wood of Lebanon — this denotes the *even shesiyah*, from which the world was established. How does the wood of Lebanon symbolize the *even shesiyah*? The Temple was partly made of Lebanon wood, and its focal point was the Holy of Holies, whose walls framed the *even shesiyah*. "The wood of Lebanon," therefore, represents the *even shesiyah*.

"He made its pillars of silver" symbolizes the chain of descent. The "gold hangings" are the fruit trees and produce of the earth, which are comparable to gold. Gold comes in many forms and hues; likewise, the land yields its crops in great variety.

"Its seat [מרכבו] purple" is a reference to God's glory, as it says, "There is none like God, Yeshurun, Who rides [רוכב] upon the Heaven as your help" (*Devarim* 33:26).

"Its inner side was decked with love" signifies the merit of the Torah and that of the righteous people whose occupation it is.

King Shlomo also alludes to the *even shesiyah* in the book of *Koheles*. He states, "I made for myself gardens and orchards, and I have planted in them every kind of fruit tree" (*Koheles* 2:5).

There is an intriguing *midrash* on this verse. The *midrash* explains that when people sow seeds in the ground sometimes they are rewarded with plants that flourish and bear fruit, and sometimes they are not. If the plants don't blossom, it is because they have not chosen the ideal location for that particular plant.

But King Shlomo was the wisest of men, and he knew exactly where to sow every seedling. The *even shesiyah* is the foundation of the world, and from it emerge numerous veins in the ground that run to different countries. Each vein has different properties suitable for different flora. He knew that Ethiopia, for example, is the center for growing peppers. Blessed with his extraordinary knowledge, Shlomo planted his pepper seeds above the vein that travels to Ethiopia, and naturally his efforts met with success. It was this aspect of his wisdom that prompted Shlomo to plant "*every* kind of fruit tree."

How King David Acquired the Site of the *Even Shesiyah*

When King David ordered his general, Yoav, to count the people, he made a major error. Counting the Jewish nation is forbidden by the Torah. The punishment for this sin was correspondingly harsh: seventy thousand people died of pestilence.

Yet it seemed even that was not sufficient. The de-

22 *Keystones of the World*

stroying angel was poised to kill the inhabitants of Jerusalem, too. But before he could carry out the divine command, God said, "Enough! Now hold back your hand" (*Divrei HaYamim* I 21:15), and the plague stopped.

At that point the destroying angel was standing by the threshing-floor of Aravna HaYevusi. The Sages of the Talmud say that God restrained the angel because He saw ashes in the granary. The granary was in the site of the *akeidah*, and the ashes were those of the ram that had been sacrificed instead of Yitzchak.

But the angel did not leave. He stayed on this spot, his sword drawn and stretched out over Jerusalem.

When David saw the angel, he fell on his face.

> David said to God, "Isn't it I who commanded the people to be counted? And it is I who have sinned and done a great wrong, but these sheep, what have they done? Hashem, my God, please let Your hand be against me and against my father's house, but not against Your people, that they should be afflicted with plague."
>
> (*Divrei HaYamim* I 21:17)

By confessing his sin and shouldering the full responsibility for the wrong he had done, David established (rather than originated) the concept of *teshuvah*, repentance. He was now fit to build the Altar and thereby lay the foundations for the Temple, whose function it is to atone for the sins of the Jewish people.

On the same day, the prophet Gad came to David, and told him, "Go up, erect an altar to God in the granary of Aravna HaYevusi" (*Shmuel* II 24:18). This altar

The Foundation Stone of the World 23

would ultimately become the Altar in the Temple. Aravna's granary, which contained the *even shesiyah*, was destined to be the area of the Temple Mount.

The Midrash comments on this verse: it is comparable to a father who strikes his son without explaining the reason for the punishment. Finally, he tells his child why he felt it necessary to hit him.

In the time of King David thousands fell in battle and died from plague. The failure to demand a Temple made them responsible for their dire fate, despite the fact that they lived before it had ever been built. So one can appreciate how culpable were those who actually witnessed the Temple and its destruction and did not clamor for its restoration. The Sages therefore ordained that the Jewish people should pray three times daily for the return of the Shechinah to Zion and the *avodah*, Temple service, to Jerusalem.

David did as he had been commanded: "David went up at the instruction of Gad, which he spoke in the Name of God" (*Divrei HaYamim* I 21:19). This ties in with the Torah's command "But in the place that God shall choose in [the territory of] one of your tribes, there you shall offer your burnt offerings..." (*Devarim* 12:14).

When Aravna saw King David, he bowed down to the ground. He offered to give David the granary and all the materials he would need to build the Altar. But David insisted on paying for everything: so "David gave to Ornan [Aravna] for the place six hundred shekels of gold by weight" (*Divrei HaYamim* I 21:25). To give all twelve tribes the opportunity to have a share in the Altar and the granary, he raised fifty shekels from each one.

24   *Keystones of the World*

The Midrash states that there are three sites the non-Jews cannot accuse us of acquiring illicitly. One is the place of the Temple, as we see in the verse quoted above. The two others are the Me'aras HaMachpeilah [see *Bereishis* 23:16] and the burial place of Yosef [see *Bereishis* 33:19].

Incidentally, this is not to say that the Land of Israel is not rightfully ours, too. The world belongs to the Creator, and He gave this land to the Jewish people. The Talmud says that a father shouldn't withhold the inheritance from a disreputable son in favor of a righteous one, as perhaps the sinner might produce worthy children. But this reasoning has no relevance in relation to God, Who is able to see the future. He therefore gave the Land of Israel to Yitzchak, Avraham's younger son, and not to Yishmael, the firstborn.

Only after he had paid the full price did David build the Altar. Sacrificing burnt offerings and peace offerings, he begged Hashem to stop the plague for good. True, the angel had been restrained from continuing his grisly work, but as long as his sword was stretched out over Jerusalem the prospect of further death still threatened the Jewish nation. Fire came down from Heaven, consuming the burnt offerings, and David understood that his prayer had been answered. The plague ceased completely, and the angel replaced the sword in its sheath. The Heavenly fire was also a sign that this place had been sanctified and would be holy forever.

Rather than traveling to the *Mishkan*, Tabernacle, in Givon, David continued to sacrifice on the altar he had built.

The Foundation Stone of the World   *25*

David said, "This is the House of Hashem, God, and this is the altar of burnt offering for Israel."

(Divrei HaYamim I 22:1)

He declared publicly, "This place in the granary is set aside as the House of God." This is comparable to what Yaakov said when he awoke from his dream: "How awesome is this place! This is none other than the House of God" (*Bereishis* 28:17).

What prompted David to make his pronouncement? Several factors. First, he saw clearly that God had responded to the prayers he had uttered on that spot — the fire descended and the plague stopped. And what had led him to sacrifice there in the first place? Nothing but God's command. Furthermore, he was still filled with terror from the sight of the angel's sword. His fearful state of mind prevented him from going to the *Mishkan* in Givon, and this was yet another significant pointer.

He therefore concluded, "This is the House of God!" May it be rebuilt speedily, in our time.

Chapter Two
Yaakov's Pillar

Yaakov went out from Be'er Sheva and went toward Charan. He came upon the place and stayed there all night, because the sun had set. And he took from the stones of the place, which he put around his head, and lay down in that place. And he dreamed, and behold a ladder.... And behold God stood by him....

Yaakov rose early in the morning and took the stone that he had put around his head and set it up as a pillar and poured oil on top of it. He called the name of that place Beis El.... And Yaakov vowed a vow, saying..."Hashem shall be my God, and this stone, which I have set up as a pillar, shall be a House of God...."

(Bereishis 28:10–22)

The Torah relates that Yaakov "took from the stones of the place." Yet seven verses later, in an apparent contradiction, the text states, "And he took the stone." Were there a number of stones or one? The Midrash resolves the difficulty, and in so doing gives us an insight into Yaakov's outlook and aspirations.

The Number of Stones

God had decreed that there would be twelve tribes who would form the basis of the Jewish nation, and Yaakov was aware of this. But he did not yet know whether he would be the one to raise them. Neither Yitzchak nor Avraham had been deemed suitable. So he took twelve stones and arranged them around his head in order to discover what would happen. Would they all unite and blend into one? If they did, this meant he would indeed be the father of twelve tribes, tribes who would be united as one.

Yaakov could equally have taken one stone to see whether it would divide into twelve. But he chose the other alternative, for two reasons. First, his aim was for the stones to join rather than split, as a sign that the tribes would be united. Second, he wanted a symbol of true union between himself and his future wives, from which would emerge the foundation of the Jewish people. And as we see from the verse, the stones did merge into one — "And he took *the stone* that he had put around his head."

According to a different explanation, Yaakov played a more passive role. He found a spot in which to pass the night and then searched for stones to put around his head. But God deliberately caused him to select a place that would have room for only twelve stones. In this manner God hinted to Yaakov that he had been chosen to raise the tribes. Moreover, the stones became one to inform him of the singular nature of the future nation — "Who is like your people, Israel, a unique nation on earth?" (*Divrei HaYamim* I 17:21).

Another *midrash* tells us that there were four stones involved here. Yaakov reasoned as follows: "My grandfather Avraham had two wives, who bore Yitzchak and Yishmael. One son was righteous and one wicked. My father, Yitzchak, had one wife and two sons, one righteous and the other wicked. If I have four wives, how many evil men will I bring into the world?" He therefore gathered four stones and waited to see if they would coalesce. Then he slept, "and he dreamed, and behold a ladder...."

When Yaakov rose in the morning, he saw that his fears were groundless. God said to him, "You are entirely beautiful, my beloved, and there is no blemish in you!" (*Shir HaShirim* 4:7). "By your life, just as these stones have become one, so all your children will be righteous" — meaning they will be as one in their righteousness.

Another opinion states that Yaakov took three stones. Both Avraham and Yitzchak were worthy of a rare distinction; their names were linked to the Creator in an association both fundamental and eternal. This occurred in their lifetime. God said, "I am the God of Avraham your father" (*Bereishis* 26:24), and Eliezer said, "Hashem, the God of my master Avraham" (ibid. 24:12). With regard to Yitzchak, Yaakov said to him, "Hashem your God caused it to happen thus before me" (ibid. 27:20).

Conscious that he was about to leave the Land of Israel and enter Lavan's house, Yaakov wanted to know if he, too, would attain this sublime level. So he decided to take three stones in order to see whether they would merge into one. It was not only that Yaakov was anxious to equal their achievements in serving God. His motive

Yaakov's Pillar
29

was deeper: he knew that if he, Avraham, and Yitzchak could, in this respect, form a threefold cord, this would bring about *hashra'as haShechinah*, the shining forth of God's Presence in the world. And we say to this very day, "The God of Avraham, the God of Yitzchak, and the God of Yaakov."

Others say that since no number is specified beyond the plural, the word מאבני ("from the stones of") signifies two stones. Since Yaakov foresaw that his wife would be the daughter of an evil man, he wished to know whether he was destined to raise unworthy offspring, like Yitzchak who also married a wicked man's daughter, and Avraham who married Hagar. Yishmael and Esav had many evil descendants, and Yaakov did not want to follow the same pattern. But why *two* stones?

The unity of the two stones indicates this self-same attribute in his children, who will walk in one path rather than traveling in two different directions. Alternatively, it means that they will be united with their father and follow in his ways. In the course of his vow, Yaakov said, "Hashem shall be my God" (*Bereishis* 28:21). This was a plea for God's Name to rest upon him in order that he should have no unworthy descendants.

All these different explanations about the actual number of stones aren't necessarily contradictory. One opinion blends two, three, and twelve stones in a single explanation. Yaakov had received blessings from Yitzchak in connection with his marriage (see *Bereishis* 28:3–4) and he was trying to discover whether they would come to fruition.

Would he raise *twelve* tribes, in fulfillment of "You

shall become a host of nations"? Would God link His Name with his own, in fulfillment of "He will give you the blessing of Avraham" (*three* stones)? Would all his children be righteous, in fulfillment of "He will give you the blessing of Avraham, to you and to your seed with you" (*two* stones)? Yaakov assembled twelve stones in total, but also included these other factors in his considerations.

Finally, the simplest solution is that Yaakov wanted to surround himself with stones, so he took several. But he actually rested his head on only one, which is why the verse states, ויקח את האבן אשר שם מראשתיו, "He took the stone that he had put at his head."

Why Stones?

So far we have dealt with the number of stones, but these same stones were also significant in a more general sense. They hinted at the fact that in the future the Jewish people would receive the Torah in the form of stone tablets. Yaakov put these "tablets of stone" מראשתיו, "around his head." מראשתיו is an expression with a further symbolic link to the Torah, which is referred to as ראשית, first, by the Talmudic Sages. That it was Yaakov who performed this action is fitting, because the *Avos* are also called ראשית, as it says, "I saw your fathers as a ripe fruit on a fig tree in its first season [בראשיתה]" (*Hoshea* 9:10).

Yaakov was, of course, fully aware of the great merit of Avraham and Yitzchak, which supported him throughout his difficult life. For example, when he prayed to God before confronting Esav, he said, "The God of my father Avraham and the God of my father Yitzchak" (*Bereishis* 32:9). This merit was encapsulated in the word, אבן, stone, which is composed of the words אב and בן, father and son.

Part of Yaakov's purpose in gathering the stones was to protect himself from being attacked by wild animals during the night. He set them around his head in the form of a gutter. But why did he shield only his head and not his body as well?

Wild animals initially attack the head, because they know instinctively that this is where the life force is concentrated. Yaakov, being aware of this, wasn't concerned about the rest of his body; he wanted to protect his brain, the most vital organ. He also bore in mind that if the beasts began to attack his body, he would feel this immediately and be able to fend them off. But if they had access to his head, they could injure him before he had the chance to rise up and battle with them.

The Midrash also tells us that the stones became as soft and comfortable as a bed and pillow. Naturally he didn't have any such items with him — he had been forced to flee from Esav, under his mother's instructions. But nature is no obstacle to its Creator, and a miracle made Yaakov's sleep pleasant. The words "He lay down in that place," which seem unnecessary, hint that he felt as comfortable as a person normally does when settling down for the night.

The Angels Quarrel

According to one opinion, the stones Yaakov had gathered began to quarrel among themselves. Each one said, "This righteous man's head should rest on me." This is meant figuratively. Angels are assigned to every inanimate object, and the angels in charge of the stones were all clamoring for this privilege.

Then the stones softened and merged into one. Why? What caused this to happen? "God stood by him" (*Bereishis* 28:13).

God appeared to Yaakov in a dream, and the stones saw His glory and melted like wax from the fire of the Divine Presence. When He merely emerges from His place, the mountains dissolve beneath Him (see *Michah* 1:3–4). It was hardly surprising, then, that the stones should melt when God stood near Yaakov, so to speak, and revealed Himself to him.

The Pillar

What is the meaning of the phrase "He took from the stones of *the place*"? Was this a place that was familiar to him?

This was the very spot where Yitzchak had almost been sacrificed in the *akeidah*, and it was well known to Yaakov. Avraham had, of course, built an altar there.

However, according to a different explanation, Yaakov was unaware at first that this was *the* place. But when he awoke he realized from the unique nature of his dream that he had been lying on holy ground, and then he understood that this was where Yitzchak had been bound. Unwittingly he had taken the stones from that altar, and he wanted to restore them to their place immediately in order not to be guilty of damaging an altar. But he discovered that there was now only one stone. Since it was no longer possible to replace what he had taken, he used the stone to build a pillar.

Yaakov anointed the pillar with a small quantity of oil that miraculously came down from Heaven, in partial fulfillment of Yitzchak's blessing, "God will give you...of the fat of the earth" (*Bereishis* 27:28). As one commentator points out, Yaakov certainly did not have any oil with him, as we know from the verse "For with my staff I passed over this Yarden" (ibid. 32:10). It therefore could have appeared only through supernatural means. But according to a different opinion, the stick with which he was traveling was hollow and contained the oil he needed.

The Sages of the Talmud tell us that Yaakov used just a modicum of oil, as much as can be held by "the lip of a jug." But from where did they derive this detail?

Later in the Torah we read, "Yaakov set up a pillar...and poured oil on it" (*Bereishis* 35:14). On that occasion he had plenty of oil and poured it over the entire pillar. But here the verse states, "He poured oil on top of it." From this the Sages infer that he covered only the top of the pillar.

Furthermore, in connection with this incident, it is written, "I am the God of Beis El, where you anointed a pillar" (ibid. 31:13). *Anointing* is used only when a small amount is involved, whereas *pouring* usually denotes a large quantity.

Intending to offer sacrifices on it when he returned, Yaakov anointed the pillar as an induction and a preparation. We see the same procedure being followed with the Mishkan and its *keilim*, vessels: "He [Moshe] had anointed them and sanctified them" (*Bemidbar* 7:1). Thus Yaakov vowed, "This stone, which I have set up as a pillar, shall be a House of God," and later it is written, "I am the God of Beis El, where you anointed a pillar."

But why was it permitted for Yaakov to make an altar from the stone he had used for a mundane purpose? A similar question can be asked about Moshe — how could he use the Midianites' ornaments to make vessels for the Mishkan?

Once the ornaments were melted down, their appearance was totally different, so they were perfectly fit to be used for a holy purpose. Likewise, the form of the stones altered. They merged into one and became as soft as a pillow. After Yaakov awoke the stone hardened in its changed form.

According to one *midrash*, this stone is still in existence. When the builders of the first Temple lifted it up along with a row of stones, it hurled itself to the ground. The stone did not want to be part of the Temple, which would later lie in ruins. So the builders cast it aside, considering it unfit for use. But King Shlomo, in his wisdom, swore that even if everything else would be destroyed, this stone would survive and remain fixed in its place. They set it in the Western Wall, and "the stone the builders had rejected became the cornerstone" (*Tehillim* 118:22).

Chapter Three
The Stone on the Mouth of the Well

An Extraordinary Feat

In *sefer Bereishis* (ch. 27) we read of how Yaakov, in mortal peril from his bloodthirsty brother, Esav, was forced to flee from his home and take refuge with his uncle Lavan. Protected only by his stick, Yaakov set out on his journey from the Land of Israel to Syria. He spent the night in Luz, and there he dreamed his supernatural dream about the ladder.

In the dream Hashem assured him, "I am with you and will guard you wherever you go" (ibid. 28:15). Yaakov was so elated by this news that, in the words of the Midrash, "his heart lifted up his feet," and he walked swiftly toward Aram:

> Then Yaakov raised his feet and went into the land of the children of the east. He looked, and behold, a well in the field. And behold, three flocks of sheep lay there beside it, for from that well they would water the flocks.
>
> Now the stone over the mouth of the well was large. When all the flocks would be assembled there, they would roll the stone from the mouth of

the well and water the sheep. Then they would put back the stone over the mouth of the well in its place....

He said [to the shepherds], "Look, it is still broad daylight; it is not yet time to bring in the livestock. Water the sheep and go on grazing." But they said, "We will be unable to until all the flocks will have been gathered and they will roll the stone off the mouth of the well. We will then water the sheep."

While he was still speaking with them, Rachel had arrived with her father's sheep, for she was a shepherdess. And it was when Yaakov saw Rachel, the daughter of Lavan, his mother's brother, and the sheep of Lavan, his mother's brother, Yaakov came forward and rolled the stone off the mouth of the well and watered the sheep of Lavan, his mother's brother.

(Bereishis 29:1–3, 7–10)

Since water was scarce, a heavy stone covered the mouth of the well. It could be moved only through the combined effort of all the shepherds and this ensured that the water was divided fairly. Once all the flocks were assembled, the shepherds would roll off the stone, water the sheep, and return the stone to its place. This was the regular order of the day.

But when Yaakov arrived, he saw three flocks lying next to the well and assumed that the shepherds were intending to take them in. "The day is still young!" he protested. "If you are hired men, you haven't finished your

The Stone on the Mouth of the Well 37

job — the sheep should still be grazed. And if they are your own animals, it's not yet time for them to be gathered."

Why did he consider it necessary to interfere?

Since Yaakov was a tzaddik, a man of integrity and truth, any kind of dishonesty was anathema to him. So he immediately spoke out and tried to right an apparent wrong.

The shepherds explained the situation to Yaakov, and during their conversation Rachel arrived with her father's sheep. When Yaakov saw her, he singlehandedly removed the heavy stone from the mouth of the well and watered Lavan's sheep.

Why does the Torah relate this incident in such detail? As one commentator explains, the stories in the Torah are not idle tales. They have great relevance and significance for later generations. Moreover, such narratives are full of precious insights and lofty thoughts; they grant us knowledge and understanding and convey important lessons.

The Nature of Yaakov's Strength

Yaakov had been learning in the yeshivah of Shem and Ever for fourteen years, and he was weary, since studying Torah saps a person's vitality. Traveling also weakens the body, and Yaakov had not been walking at an ordinary pace. But his strength nevertheless remained intact. He moved the stone from the mouth of the well as easily as one pulls a stopper from a bottle.

The shepherds found it necessary to actually roll off the stone, and the Torah therefore states, וגללו את האבן,

"They would roll the stone." Yaakov, however, merely lifted it and immediately *revealed* the well beneath; hence ויגל את האבן (from the related word גלוי, revelation).

What enabled Yaakov to perform this feat? Many shepherds were needed to tend the three flocks present, yet it was beyond their united powers to move the stone. The answer lies in the verse "Those who aspire to God shall renew their strength" (*Yeshayahu* 40:31). True fear of God strengthens and invigorates a person.

One commentator notes that the verse states, "The stone was large over the mouth of the well," and not "There was a large stone over the mouth of the well." The latter phrase would only convey that the well was covered with a big stone. But the Torah specifically says, "The stone was large," to indicate that its size was exceptional, something out of the ordinary. To move a stone of such massive proportions required divine assistance, and it was this that lay behind Yaakov's strength.

In the prayer for rain we say, יחד לב וגל אבן מפי באר מים, Yaakov united his heart to God and rolled the stone. He knew that it is God, and God alone, Who is the true repository of power, and that knowledge enabled Yaakov to move the stone unaided. It was in essence, therefore, a spiritual rather than a physical strength.

"When Yaakov Saw Rachel"

Why should the sight of Rachel impel Yaakov to move the stone? One might think he was inspired by Rachel's beauty, but the wording of the verse removes any misconceptions. "And it was when Yaakov saw Rachel, the daughter of Lavan, *his mother's brother*...." Clearly

The Stone on the Mouth of the Well   39

love for his relatives was the motivating force, and this emotion filled him with strength. Spurred by concern for their property, he removed the stone and watered "the sheep of Lavan, his mother's brother."

Another commentator says more specifically that he acted for the sake of his mother and not out of love for Rachel.

The Waters Rose

Once Yaakov had removed the stone from the well, a *midrash* relates, the waters rose of their own accord and gushed forth in abundance. A commentator depicts the scene in greater detail. As mentioned earlier, it was due to the dearth of water that the well was sealed with a stone. Since a combined effort was needed to roll off the stone, the shepherds usually waited until everyone was assembled and then divided the water fairly. So under these circumstances, why did they permit Yaakov to tend to Lavan's sheep before they were all gathered together?

Yaakov's presence caused the waters to be blessed; as soon as he removed the stone, they rose and overflowed. This explains why the verse says only, "He gave to drink." There is no mention of Yaakov drawing the water, because this was unnecessary, nor was there any need to return the stone to its place. Realizing that there was more than enough for all the flocks, the shepherds allowed Yaakov to water Lavan's sheep.

A different *midrash* points out that with regard to Yaakov it says, "He gave to drink," but about Moshe it is written, "And moreover he drew water for us" (*Shemos* 2:19). Moshe did have to draw the water, and consequently a commentator remarks, "A nail of the earlier leaders is greater than the body of the later leaders." Why are the later leaders compared to the body? People used to tie the rope of the bucket to their bodies before drawing water. Another commentator explains that whereas the nail is of minor significance, the body comprises a major part of a human being. In essence, what was trifling to the Patriarchs had greater beauty than important events in the lives of their descendants.

Upon seeing the waters rise miraculously of their own volition, Yaakov understood that God had arranged for him to meet his destined partner in this place.

The Symbolic Meaning of This Episode

The commentators emphasize that the Torah's purpose is not to tell stories. This narrative is replete with allusions to incidents in the history of the Jewish people. Every detail was carefully and precisely prepared for Yaakov, serving as a parable for the future.

The Midrash gives a number of interpretations of a widely differing nature.

Mount Sinai and the Giving of the Torah

The Midrash describes the parallel between Yaakov's experience and the giving of the Torah.

The well symbolizes Mount Sinai. It was here that the Jewish people received the Torah, which is compared to a well of living water. Just as the actual well was in a field, so too Mount Sinai was in a field in the desert.

The three flocks of sheep are an allusion to the *kohanim, levi'im,* and *yisre'eilim* who comprise the Jewish

The Stone on the Mouth of the Well   *41*

nation. When the Torah was given, the *kohanim* and *levi'im* were still one group, but the Midrash nevertheless calls the people "three flocks of sheep" since this was how they would ultimately be divided.

The shepherds would water the flocks from that well; likewise, it was through Mount Sinai that the people heard the Ten Commandments. The large stone represents the Shechinah, the Divine Presence, which descended upon the mountain.

But it was only when *all* the flocks were gathered that matters could proceed. Similarly, had one person out of the six hundred thousand been absent, the Jews would not have been able to receive the Torah. The six hundred thousand letters of the Torah correspond to the same number of souls in the Jewish nation, so everyone had to be present.

The shepherds then rolled the stone, and the Jewish nation figuratively performed the same action by causing the Shechinah to descend. It was through the medium of the Shechinah that they heard the first two commandments.

"Then they would put back the stone over the mouth of the well, in its place." The people felt that they could not survive any further direct communication from God. So they said to Moshe, "You speak with us, and we will hear, but do not let God speak with us, lest we die" (*Shemos* 20:16). The Shechinah then returned to its place. Consequently, referring to the remaining eight commandments, God said to the people, "You have seen that I have spoken with you from the heavens" (ibid., 19).

The Well in the Desert

In an alternative interpretation, the Midrash divides the verses into six sections, each of which illustrates an aspect of the well in the desert.

1. "He looked, and behold, a well in the field." The well Yaakov saw was a reflection of its counterpart in the future — the rock that traveled with the Jewish people in the desert.

2. "And behold, three flocks of sheep." This refers to the three shepherds of the flocks. Yaakov realized that the well would sustain the nation in the merit of three righteous individuals: Moshe, Aharon, and Miriam (see chapter 6). They were appointed by God to tend to the needs of the people.

3. "For from that well they would water the flocks." Each *nasi*, the leader of the tribe, would stand next to the well and draw water with his staff for his tribe and family.

4. "Now the stone over the mouth of the well was large." The traveling well was in the form of a rock, and its opening was covered with a perforated, smaller rock through which the water descended.

5. "When all the flocks would be assembled there, they would roll the stone from the mouth of the well." When the nation was encamped in the desert, the *nesi'im*, the leaders of the tribes, stood by the rock and said, "Well, arise!" And the waters obeyed their command. Figuratively, therefore, the *nesi'im* removed the stone that sealed the mouth of the well. Another commentator explains that while the people were traveling the well covered itself and rolled

The Stone on the Mouth of the Well 43

along with them. It was as if it was stopped up with a stone. But when they were stationary, the well gave of its waters, and thus, in a metaphorical sense the people rolled the stone away from the rock.

6. "Then they would put back the stone over the mouth of the well in its place." This phrase refers to the times when the nation was journeying from place to place. Then the rock would return to its former, dry state.

The Exile of Edom

A different *midrash* concentrates on two of the verses. Yaakov said to the shepherds, "Look, it is still broad daylight; it is not yet time to bring in the livestock." He saw the exile of Edom stretching out for many years. A little later, Yaakov rolled the stone from the mouth of the well. This indicates that in his merit we will emerge from this long exile.

The Synagogue and the Evil Inclination

The well also represents the synagogue, for within it is a well of living water, the holiness of the Divine Presence. The three flocks of sheep correspond to the three people who are called up to the Torah on weekdays — and "from that well," the synagogue, we hear the reading of the Torah.

The stone is an allusion to the evil inclination, as it says, "I will withdraw the heart of stone from their flesh" (*Yechezkel* 11:19). But once the congregation is gathered, the stone can be removed and the evil inclination banished. Why is this so?

44   *Keystones of the World*

According to one opinion, it is due to the Torah heard in the synagogue. As the Talmudic Sages say, if the evil inclination departs, well and good, and if not, occupy yourself with Torah.

Another commentator gives an alternative interpretation. The congregation, by virtue of its numbers, is not short of merits; in fact, it has great strength. This power enables the congregation to "roll" the evil inclination away from the synagogue, where they hear the Torah. But once the people leave, the stone returns to its place. The evil inclination promptly returns, because the congregation, having dispersed, no longer exists.

The later commentators on the Torah also draw out the symbolism inherent in this episode.

Rolling the Stone

Like the Midrash, some opinions see the stone as a metaphor for the evil inclination. One commentator points out that the word ויגל occurs twice in Tanach: once in this incident with Yaakov, and again in the verse ויגל כבודי, "And My glory rejoices" (*Tehillim* 16:9). When will ויגל כבודי be achieved? When will God's glory be revealed? With the fulfillment of ויגל את האבן — the departure of the evil inclination.

Another commentator states that the rolling of the stone, which required exceptional strength, implies that Yaakov was blessed with powerful insight and understanding and was capable of clarifying profound and esoteric concepts.

Furthermore, the power of prayer is linked to the verse "And they would roll the stone." Such is the force

The Blessing of Children

of prayer, that it can change the attribute of justice to the attribute of mercy. Once the stone has been pushed aside through sincere supplication, God's kindness can pour forth in abundance.

The Blessing of Children

This incident also conveys a number of significant facts about Yaakov's marriage and the lives of the Patriarchs and Matriarchs.

"He looked, and behold, a well in the field." Rivkah was tested through a well and consequently was considered worthy of marrying Yitzchak. So when Yaakov came across a well in a field, he understood that this symbolized a wife and saw it as a favorable portent for his own marriage.

"Three flocks of sheep lay there beside it." This hints at the Patriarchs, Avraham, Yitzchak, and Yaakov. They all chose wives from the "well" in Charan, by marrying into the same prestigious family.

"For from that well they would water the flocks" — these are the children the wives bore their husbands. But the blessing of children was not easily earned, "and the stone was large upon the mouth of the well." Barrenness afflicted the women of that particular family. All four matriarchs were barren by nature, including Leah, about whom the verse says, "He opened her womb" (*Bereishis* 29:31).

However, "when all the flocks would be assembled there, they would roll the stone from the mouth of the well." The Patriarchs, through their numerous merits and heartfelt prayers, succeeded in removing this barrier. Throughout the relevant chapters in *Bereishis*, we see how the stone repeatedly returned to the mouth of the well. Sarah eventually bore Yitzchak, but then Rivkah found herself in a similar predicament. In the merit of Avraham and Yitzchak, she bore twins, Yaakov and Esav, but later Rachel suffered in the same manner. When Yaakov rolled the stone, he realized that he too would be able to dispel Rachel's barrenness, and children would be granted to them. Hence, "he watered the sheep." And what of Yaakov's daughters-in-law? He did not return the stone to its place, and they were entirely free from this problem.

Exile and Redemption

A further insight into this episode is provided by a dialogue related in the Talmud. Some Sages from Athens posed a question to the *Tanna* Rabbi Yehoshua: "We have a well in a field, and we want to bring it into the city. How should we go about it?"

Rabbi Yehoshua answered, "Make some ropes out of bran, and use these ropes to pull the well into the city."

What is the meaning behind this exchange?

The abundant flow of goodness that emanates from God is called a well of living water, as it is written, "They have forsaken Me, the fountain of living waters" (*Yirmeyahu* 2:13).

When the Jewish people lived in their own country, the "well" resided in the "city," in the Land of Israel. But once the nation was in exile together with the Shechinah, the Divine Presence, the well was no longer in the city; it had departed from its place and had moved to a field. So the Sages asked Rabbi Yehoshua, "How can we bring the well back to the city? What will encourage the Shechinah to return to Zion?"

The Stone on the Mouth of the Well 47

With his answer, Rabbi Yehoshua implied that the main cause of exile is the baseless hatred people bear for one another. The Jews have not been redeemed because they are similar to bran and other waste materials that cannot cohere to form one rope. Accordingly, Rabbi Yehoshua gave a piece of sarcastic advice in order to convey his point: make some ropes from bran!

The well in the field, therefore, denotes exile. The three flocks of sheep lying next to the well correspond to the three exiles that forced the Jewish people to leave their land: Egypt, Babylon, and Edom. In exile, too, it is solely "from that well" that the flocks are nourished; our existence is totally dependent on divine providence and the flow of God's bounty. But "the stone is large upon the mouth of the well." Sins and the evil inclination cover the well, sealing access to the waters of salvation. It is only when the Jews repent and "gather together" within their exile that they can roll away the stone and reveal the Source. But this is far from being a satisfactory situation. The people revert to their sins, and as a result the stone returns to its place.

This pattern will continue until "Yaakov draws near"; in his merit the Temple will be rebuilt, as God indicated to him after his dream. The stones he had placed around his head merged into one, signifying the ultimate true unity of the Jewish nation. The time will come when Rachel approaches with the flock of sheep, the holy nation of Israel, and Yaakov will roll the stone from the mouth of the well for all eternity.

Chapter Four
The Stone of Israel

Yaakov Avinu was old. He had reached the age of 147 and for seventeen years had been living amid the physical comforts of Egypt. He had been reunited with his favorite son, Yosef, and now, on his deathbed, summoned him and his other sons, as it is written, "Gather together and listen, sons of Yaakov; and listen to Israel your father" (*Bereishis* 49:2). Then he blessed each of them. The following verse is part of Yaakov's blessing to Yosef:

> His bow was strongly established, and the arms of his hands were made golden by the hands of the Mighty One of Yaakov; **from there he became the sustainer of the stone of Israel [משם רועה אבן ישראל].**

> (*Bereishis* 49:24)

The phrase "the stone of Israel" is somewhat enigmatic. Was Yaakov referring to himself? To Yosef? The commentators shed light on Yaakov's words.

Yaakov and His Family

To place the phrase in its setting, we will begin with an interpretation that explains the meaning of the whole verse.

The Stone of Israel

49

"His bow" is a symbol of power. Yosef's position as viceroy of Egypt was firmly established and in no danger of being undermined. "His hands were made golden" when the king presented his signet ring to Yosef. But what caused Yosef to shoot to power? Who engineered this amazing chain of events? The Almighty, the God of Yaakov. And "from there" through his position as viceroy, Yosef sustained and supported the "stone of Israel," Yaakov. As the founder of the tribes of Israel, Yaakov is given this title.

A number of commentators state that the "stone of Israel" refers not just to Yaakov, but to his sons as well. According to one view, אבן, stone, is an abbreviation of אב and בן, father and son, for Yosef sustained both his father and his brothers.

In a similar vein, another commentator explains that the word אבן means אב, father, and denotes both the father Yaakov and his family.

"The sustainer" has a double significance. It was God, Who nourished Yaakov and his family by promoting Yosef to the position of viceroy. Furthermore, it was Yosef, who tended to the needs of his father and brothers.

An alternative interpretation of the entire verse (and the preceding one) is as follows: At a certain period in his youth, Yosef's brothers embittered his life and hated him. But he remained strong, and "his arms" didn't weaken because he listened to God. He was the powerful son of Yaakov, so it was he who supported his family.

The infant nation of Israel was then like an inanimate stone, states another commentator. Apart from

50   *Keystones of the World*

Yosef, none of the brothers had any experience of trade. Naturally it fell to him to provide for his family and succor "the stone, Israel."

Yosef

The Talmud relates that when Yosef was tempted to sin with Potifar's wife the image of his father appeared to him in the window. Yaakov said to his son, "Yosef! In the future your name and those of your brothers will be engraved on the stones of the *eifod* (one of the *kohen gadol's* vestments). Do you want yours to be blotted out? Do you want to be described as ורועה זונות, 'one who associates with immoral women' (*Mishlei* 29:3)?"

Upon hearing these words, Yosef conquered his evil inclination. Thus it was "the might of Yaakov" that caused Yosef's name to be engraved on the stone of the *eifod*. And "from there he became a shepherd, a stone of Israel." (This interpretation renders the word רועה as "shepherd" rather than "sustainer.") Since he remained righteous, he was deemed worthy of being a shepherd for his people.

One commentator focuses on the word משם: "*from there* he became the sustainer, the stone of Israel." שם, there, is connected to the word שממה, desolation and emptiness. From being desolate and despondent, Yosef became a "sustainer" whose wisdom nurtured the people of Egypt. But it was not only the Egyptians who benefited from his presence. It was Yosef's privilege to be the stone of Israel. Just as a cornerstone maintains the two adjoining walls, so he supported his father and his entire family.

Alternatively, שם is a rare singular form of שמים, the heavens. At the very highest celestial level, it was arranged that Yosef would sustain his family in particular and the country in general. He thus attained the title of "the stone of Israel."

The Jewish People

Setting this phrase in a broader context, several commentators conclude that "the stone" refers to the Jewish people.

The Sages of the Talmud say that *knesses Yisrael*, the assembly of Israel, represents the אבן הראשה, the keystone of the universe. "The stone, Israel," therefore, denotes the object that completes the structure of the world.

In Midrashic literature, there are many allusions to stones that are symbolic of the Jewish nation.

In *Koheles* we read, "To everything there is a season...a time to gather stones together" (*Koheles* 3:1, 5). A *midrash* explains that this verse refers to two major events in Jewish history. The first is the splitting of the Red Sea. In the words of King David, "He caused Israel to pass through its [the Red Sea's] midst" (*Tehillim* 136:14). In this instance, the Jewish people, symbolized by stones, were *gathered* to safety by dint of an open miracle.

The second occasion referred to in *Koheles* is *mattan Torah*, the giving of the Torah, when the people assembled around Mount Sinai in accordance with God's instructions.

The *Midrash Rabbah* quotes a verse from *Mishlei*: כובד אבן ונטל החול, "A stone is heavy and the sand weighty" (*Mishlei* 27:3). God says: "I have *honored* [כבדתי] Israel who is called a stone," as it is written, אבן ישראל, "the stone, Israel." Since the world was created for the sake of the Jewish people, they are compared to the foundation stone and the cornerstone and are honored accordingly by God.

A different *midrash* states that the gentile nations are compared to pottery. It is written, "When you come to the land, which Hashem your God gives you, you shall not learn to do like the abominations of those nations. There shall not be found among you anyone who makes his son or his daughter pass through the fire" (*Devarim* 18:9–10). Since the gentiles were in the habit of killing their children in this manner, they are likened to pottery, which also passes through fire.

Yaakov, however, is called a "stone." The Midrash illustrates the relationship between the Jews and the gentiles with the following analogy: if a pot falls on a rock, it is the pot that shatters. Likewise, when the gentiles attack the Jewish people, it is the former who will truly suffer.

Finally, a beautiful interpretation of the whole phrase, משם רועה אבן ישראל ("From there he became the sustainer of the stone of Israel"). This commentator gives an interesting translation of the word רועה: to immerse oneself in deep thought over a period of time (connecting רועה to the word רעיון, thought). When the Jewish people are in exile, they are similar to dust, as it is written, "Your children shall be like the dust of the earth" (*Bereishis* 28:14). The gentiles are compared to water, as it says, "Ah, the uproar of many peoples...and the rushing

The Stone of Israel

of nations that rush like the rushing of mighty waters!" (*Yeshayahu* 17:12). The powerful waters flow onto the specks of dust, dissolving them until they are completely lost. But when the particles coalesce and form a solid stone, even a torrent of water cannot destroy it.

The exiled Jewish people hold their fate in their own hands. If diverse opinions truly divide, every individual is as a speck of dust, vulnerable to attack by hostile enemies. But if they bond together and become "the stone, Israel," no force can harm them.

"The might of Yaakov" represents the kindness and love of peace that were an integral part of Yaakov, qualities he bequeathed to Yosef. The verse continues, משם רועה אבן ישראל. It is this trait, this desire to bestow kindness, that bears important consequences. Yosef in particular, and the Jewish people in general, will think deeply about how to unite our nation and bring about the emergence of "the stone, Israel."

Chapter Five

The Tablets

God said to Moshe, "Come up to Me, to the mountain, and be there; and I will give you the *tablets of stone*, and the Torah and the commandment, which I have written, that you may teach them"....

Moshe entered into the midst of the cloud and went up to the mountain; and Moshe was in the mountain forty days and forty nights....

He gave to Moshe, when He had finished speaking with him upon Mount Sinai, the two tablets of the testimony, *tablets of stone*, written with the finger of God.

(*Shemos* 24:12, 24:18, 31:18)

For forty days and nights, Moshe labored to absorb the Torah. Even he did not find this task easy, for he could not retain what he had learned. The Sages say he studied and then forgot. At the end of this period, the Midrash continues, God gave Moshe the Torah as a present.

A commentator explains that forty days were needed for Moshe's mind to become separated from the material world. During this period he ate no food, but was nourished with "the bread of the mighty," a spiritual sustenance that also nurtured the angels. But even on the

The brain corresponds to the *luchos*, the tablets. It, too, is divided into two parts. Although these human "*luchos*" are of flesh and blood, they can nevertheless soar to great heights by being immersed solely in the spiritual.

thirty-ninth day, Moshe was still not free from physical connections, and consequently he still forgot his learning. By the end of forty days, however, his mind was akin to an angel's; there was no need for him to listen and learn, for he grasped every concept even before it had been explained.

The brain corresponds to the *luchos*, the tablets. It, too, is divided into two parts. Although these human "*luchos*" are of flesh and blood, they can nevertheless soar to great heights by being immersed solely in the spiritual.

"Tablets of Stone"

Unlike the second *luchos*, these were the handiwork of God Himself. Hewn from beneath the Throne of Glory, they were made of sapphire, a brilliant blue stone. We learn of their origin from the verse. According to the system of *at-bash* (see glossary), the letters of לחת, tablets, correspond to those of כסא, throne. And just as the Divine Presence rests on the Throne of Glory, so too it rested upon the *luchos*.

Why were they made of stone rather than any other material? The Midrash says that the *luchos* were given in the merit of our forefather Yaakov, who is called "the stone of Israel" (see chapter 4). Since Yaakov sacrificed himself for Torah by learning day and night, his descendants received the *luchos* in his merit.

"Two Tablets"

According to the Sages of the Talmud, each tablet

56   *Keystones of the World*

was six handbreadths long, six handbreadths wide, and three handbreadths thick. The shorter spelling, לחת, rather than לחות, implies a singular form, hinting that they were of uniform size and weight. This was a miracle in itself, for a human being is incapable of making two objects of precisely the same measurements.

Neither tablet was larger than the other, and, correspondingly, the commandments between man and God are no more and no less important than those between man and his friend. We cannot truly fulfill the former without the latter and vice versa. Our natural environment is within a community, and we supply each other's needs in numerous ways. Moreover, the world cannot continue without marriage. Within this framework, the interpersonal commandments provide a training ground for our duties toward God, for it is far easier to act altruistically toward a human being than toward God, who cannot be seen.

The converse is also true. Once a person recognizes that his fellow man has been created in the image of God, he feels bound to act kindly toward him.

The two *luchos* also correspond to heaven and earth, bridegroom and bride, the two *unterferers* (who accompany the bride and groom to the wedding ceremony), and this world and the hereafter.

Torah is the essence of creation; without it, heaven and earth would not have been founded. It is written, "If it were not for My covenant, I would not have fixed day and night, the ordinances of heaven and earth" (*Yirmeyahu* 33:25). On one tablet were inscribed the commandments between man and God; for their sake the

The Tablets   57

heavens were created. The other tablet contained the interpersonal commandments for which the earth was formed.

They also symbolize a bridegroom and bride. One tablet represents God, the Bridegroom, and the other the Jewish people, the bride.

The *unterferers* act as intermediaries by bringing together the groom and bride. The *luchos* — the Torah — play a similar role by uniting the Jewish people to their Father in Heaven.

Finally, the tablets also correspond to this world and the hereafter. Through the Torah one gains both worlds.

"Tablets of the Testimony"

Why are the *luchos* given this appellation?

The Jewish nation had heard the Ten Commandments at Sinai, and the tablets were a written testimony of their experience. Furthermore, they are so described because they were written not on one tablet but on two — viable testimony requires at least two witnesses.

Another opinion connects the word העדות, "the testimony" to יעד, "he promised." God had promised Moshe, "I will give you the tablets of stone" (*Shemos* 24:12). But the people sinned grievously by making the golden calf, whereupon God said to Moshe, "Go, go down, for your people have acted corruptly" (ibid. 32:7).

According to a *midrash*, the *luchos* testified that the Divine Presence rested among the people, for they were akin to the personal signet of the King.

"Written with the Finger of God"

How can we understand this phrase?

The Torah uses the limbs of the body as metaphors for their functions. The foot is associated with movement; the lip signifies speech. And in connection with the *luchos*, the finger indicates a divine act.

According to another commentator, the phrase denotes a work of wondrous craftsmanship, comparable to the verse "When I behold Your heavens, the work of Your fingers..." (*Tehillim* 8:4). The letters on the *luchos* were all hewn in one instant, unlike human writing, which is completed in stages.

One commentator explains that God drew the shape of each letter with the divine light, which was in the form of a finger. This light was directed onto the *luchos*.

If the *luchos* were in a purely spiritual form, how could Moshe hold them in his hand? Alternatively, if they were solid physical objects, how was it possible for God to give them to Moshe?

In Heaven, the *luchos* had no connection at all to the material world, but when they were brought down to Mount Sinai, they were enveloped in a physical cloak. We can now understand both how Moshe could receive the *luchos* and how God could pass them to Moshe. The soul within man gives life and movement — the body is merely the outer casing. Similarly, the Godly writing was the soul of the *luchos*, the stone the necessary physical element. Due to the dual nature of the tablets, they could be transferred from God to Moshe, as it is written, "And He gave to Moshe...the two tablets of the testimony."

The first words of the next verse signal the catastrophe that was about to befall the Jewish nation. "When the people saw that Moshe delayed coming down from the mountain..." Forty days after receiving the Torah, they deified a golden calf, so powerful was the lure of idol worship.

This sin almost spelled the end of the existence of the Jewish people. God was about to destroy them and start afresh with Moshe: "I will consume them, and I will make you into a great nation" (*Shemos* 32:10). But Moshe begged God to reconsider His words, and these prayers were accepted. He then descended the mountain with the *luchos* in his hand.

> And Moshe turned and went down from the mountain, and the two tablets of the testimony were in his hand. The tablets were written on both their sides; on the one side and on the other they were written. And the tablets were the work of God, and the writing was the writing of God, engraved upon the tablets.
>
> (*Shemos* 32:15–16)

The Two Sides of the *Luchos*

The Sages of the Talmud explain that the writing penetrated the stone from one side to the other. Nevertheless, by dint of a miracle, the letters were not inverted; on either side the commandments could be read in the normal manner. Furthermore, the stone material at the

60   *Keystones of the World*

center of the ם (*mem sofit*) and ס (*samech*) remained suspended, in obedience to the will of the Creator.

A commentator links these two miracles to the phrase "the tablets of the testimony." Jewish law requires at least two witnesses when evidence has to be proven. These supernatural phenomena testify that the writing was none other than that of God.

A verse in the book of *Esther* gives us a more profound understanding of the message conveyed by the two miracles. It is written, "Then Esther summoned Hasach...and ordered him to go to Mordechai, to learn what this was about and why [מה זה ועל מה זה]" (*Esther* 4:5). The Talmud explains that Esther sent a message to Mordechai: "Perhaps they [the Jewish people] have transgressed the five books of the Torah, in which it says, מזה ומזה הם כתובים, 'On the one side and the other they were written.' "

What did Esther mean? And how was her concern bound up with the inscription on the *luchos*?

Mordechai forbade the people to attend the royal banquet, but they went nevertheless and were guilty of eating *bishul akum*, food cooked by a gentile. But why were they threatened with such a harsh punishment — total destruction — for violating a rabbinical prohibition? And if their only sin was to eat at the banquet, it seems that in their own homes they adhered to the dietary laws. In that case, why did they disobey Mordechai?

Mordechai's generation mistakenly thought that it is permissible to be lenient with many of the mitzvos while in exile. Since they were under gentile rule, they imag-

The Tablets 61

ined they were free from some of the restrictions that separated them from the non-Jews. "If we are the only nation that is not at the banquet, the king will become enraged," they reasoned. "He will see us as traitors and pass anti-Jewish laws." In view of this danger, they allowed themselves to eat the non-kosher food but continued to observe the dietary laws scrupulously at home.

The Torah does not apply only within a specific set of circumstances. It was the blueprint for the creation of the world and is binding in every country and at all times. In order to convey the eternity of the Torah, the engraving on the *luchos* pierced the stone from side to side. Had the letters been only partially engraved or written with ink, the inscription could have been erased with the passage of time. In addition, the stone at the center of the *mem* and *samech* miraculously remained in place. Limited by our puny reasoning, we cannot understand how it is possible to fulfill the whole Torah in every era and continent, under the most trying and difficult of circumstances. But we know that the words of the Torah last forever and exist beyond nature, in the realm of the supernatural.

The phrase מזה ומזה הם כתובים, "On the one side and on the other they were written," hints at two additional points. The Ten Commandments were written on both sides of the *luchos*; from either direction, the words read exactly the same. Likewise, wherever the Jewish people are scattered, the Torah can be read without any alteration at all. Furthermore, we must fulfill the mitzvos "within and without." It is not enough for our hearts to be turned to Heaven — our actions must match our inner

62   *Keystones of the World*

convictions. But at the time of Achashveirosh, the Jewish people were guilty of ignoring this principle.

The Work and the Writing of God

Why at this point, just prior to the shattering of the *luchos*, does the Torah stress, "The tablets were the work of God, and the writing was the writing of God"? When Moshe beheld the spectacle of the people serving the golden calf, he was so appalled that he broke the *luchos* despite these unique qualities.

There is another reason for mentioning the "writing of God" at this juncture. When Moshe entered the vicinity of the golden calf, with its inherent impurity and sin, the holy letters flew up from the *luchos* and departed.

The *luchos* were "the work of God." It was the divine speech that had formed the tablets, just as it had created the heavens, as it is written, "By the word of God the heavens were made" (*Tehillim* 33:6). We read in the Mishnah, "Ten things were created on the eve of Shabbos, at twilight [one of which is] the *luchos*" (*Avos* 5:8). Each one was a miraculous phenomenon in its own right and remained as it had been created until its time came.

The Midrash states that every day a *bas kol*, a Heavenly voice, emanates from Mount Chorev, saying, "Woe to people for the insult to the Torah!" Anyone who isn't constantly occupied with Torah is rebuked by God, as it is written, "The tablets were the work of God."

A commentator explains that the Torah was given on Mount Chorev, which is another name for Sinai. The *bas kol* mentioned in the Midrash is not to be taken literally — when the Jewish people are not taken up with learning Torah, it is considered as if Mount Sinai is making this declaration. But why is their behavior described in such strong terms?

If they truly valued Torah, they would not neglect it; this lack of esteem is considered an insult. And as a result people bring all kinds of suffering upon themselves.

The Torah is infinitely precious to God. Just as a dedicated craftsman is constantly busy with his beloved work, God's delight lies only in Torah, and He expects His children to continually delve into its treasures.

"Engraved upon the Tablets"

The meaning of the phrase חרות על הלוחות is explored at length by the commentators.

According to one opinion, the word "engraved," which indicates physical labor, cannot be the correct translation in connection with divine writing. Moreover, the verse says "upon the tablets," and any engraving would of necessity be within the tablets.

The commentator explains that the word חרות is connected to חור, hole, which in this context is used in a spiritual rather than a physical sense. The hole opened something that was formerly closed. Whereas previously the two sides of the *luchos* were sealed together, the hole now created a distinction and a separation, which clarified the entire Torah. Both in origin and meaning, פרישות, separation, is linked to the word פירוש, explanation. God's writing was clearly expressed upon the *luchos*, to the extent that everyone could understand its inner meaning.

64   *Keystones of the World*

One can now appreciate why such great preparation was necessary for the giving of the Torah. The Ten Commandments contained far more than ten laws that are easily grasped and accepted by any sensible person. Included within them was detail upon detail — in fact, all 613 mitzvos as they are explained in the Oral Law. These were no simple commandments, and consequently Moshe stayed on the mountain for forty days and nights before descending with the *luchos*.

But one might wonder how such a feat was accomplished. How could the tablets contain the entire written and oral law? The answer lies in the words "the writing of God." God has unlimited power and ability. He placed the Torah on the *luchos*, and He prepared the inscription in a lucid, comprehensible form so that each law and *midrash* was crystal clear. Since the Jewish people were on a lofty spiritual level, they were capable of understanding the Torah in this setting.

The Talmud says that had the first *luchos* not been shattered, Torah would not have been forgotten from Israel. The entire Torah was explained on the tablets, and this complete knowledge would have served all future generations as well.

The Midrash says, "Don't read this word as *charus*, engraved, but as *cheirus*, freedom." A commentator explains that the Midrash is answering an obvious question. Why does the Torah say, חרות על הלוחות, "engraved *above* the tablets," and not בלוחות, "*in* the tablets"? Can one engrave in the air, above the tablets? The Talmudic Sages infer that the Jewish people were about to gain

The Tablets

freedom, על הלוחות, *because* of the *luchos* — in the merit of the Torah.

But what is meant by "freedom"? The Midrash states three opinions: release from exile, from the Angel of Death, and from suffering. If the Angel of Death would protest to God, "You have created me for nothing!" God would reply, "I have given you power over every nation in the world, except one — to whom I have granted freedom."

A commentator explains that the commandments emanating from God took on a physical form and were placed above the tablets. The letters remained suspended there, "free above the *luchos*," for they weren't subjugated to the stone tablets at all. When the *luchos* were shattered, the letters flew away (they were later used for the second tablets).

Correspondingly, all those who studied Torah would also have been free men — free from exile, suffering, and death. And while the first *luchos* remained intact a covenant existed to this effect. But after the sin of the golden calf, they no longer deserved these promises, so Moshe broke the *luchos*, as it is written, "I said, 'You are divine beings, and all of you sons of the Most High. But you shall die like men' " (*Tehillim* 82:6–7). Because of their sin, they lost the gift of immortality.

❀   ❀   ❀

Moshe Shatters the Tablets

And it came to pass, as soon as he approached the camp, that he saw the calf and the dancing, and Moshe's wrath glowed, and he cast the tablets out

Keystones of the World

of his hands and broke them beneath the mountain.

(Shemos 32:19)

When the Torah was given, Moshe had built an altar at the foot of the mountain, sealing the covenant between God and the Jewish people (see *Shemos* 23:4). This was the place where he now threw down the *luchos*.

Moshe was not carrying out a divine command. He shattered the *luchos* of his own accord. But his deed met with the full approval of God, as is indicated by a later verse: Hashem said to Moshe, "...the first tablets that you have broken [אשר שברת]" (ibid. 34:1). Surely Moshe was aware of what he had done. But the use of the word אשר hints at אישור, affirmation, and indicates that God endorsed his action.

Why was such a drastic act necessary?

The people considered the calf a vehicle for Godliness; they were completely immersed in idol worship. Had Moshe presented them with the *luchos*, these would have been seized on as objects for idolatry — the calf would have been exchanged for the tablets. But Moshe shattered the *luchos*, and this brought them to their senses. They realized that they had not achieved belief in God and His Torah.

The Midrash says Moshe reasoned as follows: "The paschal offering is only a single mitzvah, but it was not given to idol worshipers (as it is written, 'No stranger shall eat of it' — *Shemos* 12:43). So surely I should not give the whole of the Torah to idol worshipers?" Whereupon he broke the *luchos*.

The Tablets 67

The Midrash explains further that Moshe realized the Jewish people deserved to be destroyed, so he looked for an excuse to save them. "It says on the *luchos*, 'He who sacrifices to the gods shall be doomed to death' (*Shemos* 22:19)," Moshe thought. "Until now they weren't aware of the punishment for idol worship, for had they known, they wouldn't have made the calf. I'll break the *luchos* [as a symbolic gesture] and then speak to God, submitting this defense."

According to a different explanation, Moshe broke the *luchos* because he wanted to be regarded as a sinner. God would no longer be able to say, "I will consume them, and I will make you into a great nation" (*Shemos* 32:10), for he and the people were equally guilty. After Moshe had shattered the *luchos*, he said to God, "If You forgive them, all is well. But if not, You will not grant me forgiveness either. Therefore please blot me out from Your book."

The Timing

While Moshe was still on Mount Sinai, he was told of the terrible sin perpetrated by the Jewish nation: "They have made for themselves a molten calf and have bowed down to it..." (*Shemos* 32:8). Why didn't Moshe smash the *luchos* there and then?

The people had been waiting for Moshe to descend from the mountain, and he wanted to show them why he had been away for so long. The *luchos* were the reason.

Another commentator quotes Moshe's words "I broke them before your eyes" (*Devarim* 9:17). Something a person sees with his own eyes makes a profound im-

68 *Keystones of the World*

pression. Had Moshe merely told them that he had broken the *luchos*, they would not have felt their loss so deeply.

In a similar vein, a commentator explains that by shattering the tablets Moshe in effect took the Torah away from the people. They cried, "What have you done to us? We want the Torah back!" This heartfelt cry was a merit for the Jewish people and marked the beginning of the atonement process.

The Nature of the Sin

Other commentators place more emphasis on the nature of the sin. According to one opinion, Moshe misunderstood the people's motives. He thought they had made the calf as a replacement for himself, a subsitute for the leader who had still not returned. Surely, once they would see him, they would stop this folly and repent. But Moshe's appearance did not have the desired effect; the people continued dancing and worshiping the calf. Now Moshe realized that they were truly rebelling against God and His servant. The calf was not just a figurehead but an idol! At that point he grew angry and shattered the *luchos*.

A different commentator stresses the joy with which they performed the sin. Moshe had hoped that the people would be able to recover their purity and thus be fit to receive the *luchos*. But when he saw them dancing around the calf, he despaired, for they had made a virtue out of their iniquity and were reveling in their wrongdoing. Joy expresses a person's deepest feelings, and Moshe now became aware of the true character of this sin.

The Tablets 69

How did Moshe react when God told him what the people had done? The Midrash says that he seized the *luchos* and would not believe it. He said, "What I don't see I don't believe." He didn't break the *luchos* until he himself saw them serving the calf, as it says, "And it came to pass as he approached the camp, and he saw the calf...and he cast the tablets out of his hands" (*Shemos* 32:19).

But how could Moshe disbelieve God? Moshe assumed the people had sinned in thought only. He could not credit the fact that they had literally worshiped an idol and concluded that God's words expressed the severity of His displeasure. For a sin on this smaller scale, they did not deserve to to be deprived of the *luchos*.

In this connection, the Midrash issues a warning. Woe to people who bear witness to what they have not seen! Moshe didn't believe the simple meaning of God's words and judged the people favorably. How much more so are we obliged to restrict our evidence to what we have seen and not rely on hearsay.

The Midrash also brings a different explanation. Moshe did believe the literal meaning of God's words, but he wanted to teach the people a lesson in proper conduct. Even if you hear something untoward from a reliable individual, it is forbidden to act on this information unless you have seen it yourself.

The Writing

How could Moshe shatter the *luchos*, which contained the Name of God? Wasn't this tantamount to erasing His Name? Furthermore, it's difficult to understand why Moshe, as God's faithful servant, did not return the *luchos* to God and ask what was to be done with them.

It is analogous to a king who sends forth a proclamation in his own hand, sealed with his personal seal, in the trust of his loyal servant. If the princes don't want to accept it, the servant should return the gift forthwith. He should certainly not tear it up.

But when Moshe approached the camp, the site of idol worship, the writing flew up and returned to its source. The soulless *luchos* were heavy, and he had to hold them with both hands. Their holiness had departed, and he shattered them.

It is interesting to note that the *luchos* are referred to as "the tablets of the testimony" or "the tablets of the covenant," but when Moshe broke them, they were merely called "the tablets." It was the writing that represented the testimony and the covenant.

❀   ❀   ❀

The Second *Luchos*

The *luchos* lay in pieces, but all was not lost. Moshe continued to plead for forgiveness, and ultimately God said, "Hew for yourself two tablets of stone" (*Shemos* 34:1). God thereby indicated to Moshe that He was no longer angry with the Jewish people.

> God said to Moshe, "Hew for yourself two tablets of stone like the first ones, and I will write upon the tablets the words that were on the first tablets, which you broke. And be ready by the morning and

The Tablets   *71*

come up in the morning to Mount Sinai, and present yourself there to Me on the top of the mountain. And no man shall come up with you, nor let any man be seen throughout all the mountain, nor let the flocks or herds feed before that mountain."

He hewed two tablets of stone like the first ones, and Moshe rose early in the morning and went up to Mount Sinai, as God had commanded him, and took in his hand two tablets of stone. God descended in the cloud...and He proclaimed, "Hashem, Hashem, God, merciful and gracious...."

He was there with God forty days and forty nights; he neither ate bread nor drank water. And He wrote upon the tablets the words of the covenant, the Ten Commandments.

(Shemos 34:1–6, 28)

"Hew for Yourself..."

Moshe had prayed fervently on behalf of the Jewish people, but until this point God had not mentioned the *luchos* at all. Moshe therefore assumed that they would not be replaced. But now he was told that since he had broken them he was obliged to prepare new ones: *"Hew for yourself* two tablets of stone...on the first tablets, which you broke" — hew in order to fulfill your duty and replace what you have destroyed. The first *luchos* were made of stone, so these too had to be made of stone.

The Midrash illustrates this with a parable. A king traveled overseas and left his betrothed in the charge of the maidservants. But due to their immoral behavior, her reputation suffered. What was to be done? The bride's

72 — *Keystones of the World*

friend had an idea: he would tear up her *kesubah*, her marriage contract. *If the king wants to kill her*, the friend thought, *I'll tell him that she is not yet his wife.* The deed was done — the *kesubah* was torn up and the evidence destroyed.

When the king returned home, he made a careful investigation and discovered that only the maidservants were guilty. Then he was reconciled with his bride.

Subsequently the bride's friend said to the king, "Please write her another *kesubah* — the first one was torn up."

The king replied, "You were responsible for that deed. You buy a fresh sheet of paper, and I will write out the *kesubah* for my bride."

The king represents God, and the maidservants the *eirev rav*, the Egyptians who had attached themselves to the people when they left Egypt. The bride's friend is Moshe, and God's betrothed is the Jewish nation.

Elsewhere in the Midrash we read a well-known verse from *Koheles*: "There is a time to cast away stones..." (*Koheles* 3:5). This corresponds to the shattering of the *luchos* — "And Moshe's wrath glowed, and he cast the tablets from his hands" (*Shemos* 32:19). The verse in *Koheles* continues, "...and a time to gather stones together." Later in the parashah we read, "God said to Moshe, 'Hew for yourself two tablets of stone....' " Since there is a time to cast away stones, there is a time to gather them — one causes the other. Similarly, "There is a time to be born and a time to die" — birth leads to death.

The second *luchos*, like the first, were made of sapphire. But how did Moshe obtain this rare stone? God

The Tablets

showed him a quarry of sapphire in his tent and said, פסל לך, "Hew for yourself," indicating that הפסולת שלך, "the chippings are yours." These chippings made Moshe wealthy. We learn from here that anyone who occupies himself with Torah is thereby provided with his worldly needs. Moshe didn't have to travel to find wealth — God prepared his means of support in his own tent.

God said, "It is just and fair that Moshe should take these chippings. The Jewish people (at the time of the Exodus) were not engaged in doing mitzvos, and I gave them all the good of the land of Egypt. It was Moshe who sought out Yosef's body for reburial — is it fair that he should be poor? I will give him the chippings, and he will become wealthy."

Had Moshe not broken the *luchos*, Hashem would have provided him with riches in a different manner. But why did God want him to be wealthy? Affluence lends authority, and it was necessary for Moshe's words to be obeyed. Furthermore, people have respect for someone who is independent and not reliant on others for his needs. His wealth also enabled him to fulfill Torah and mitzvos with a munificence that befitted the great leader.

Further Instructions

Moshe was commanded to hew two tablets and be ready to ascend the mountain by the following morning. Before the Shechinah descended on Mount Sinai for the benefit of the Jewish people, three days' preparation were required. But now Moshe himself needed only one day.

He was instructed to stand on top of the mountain

Keystones of the World

and wait for God in that place: ונצבת לי שם, "Present yourself there to Me." The word לי, "to Me," has the numerical value of forty, hinting at the number of days Moshe would be there.

The verse says, "And be ready by the morning, and come up in the morning." What does the repetition signify? God was telling Moshe, "Be ready in the morning in order to receive the attribute of the morning." The quality of mercy is prevalent in the early hours of the day, as it is written, "God, in the morning You will hear my voice; in the morning I will order my prayer to you and will look forward" (*Tehillim* 5:4).

An additional directive was that Moshe was to go alone. When Moshe ascended the mountain for the first *luchos*, he was accompanied by the Elders, and the people had been warned that neither they nor their animals were allowed to touch the mountain. Now this prohibition was extended: the area of the mountain was out of bounds for man and beast. Why were these new restrictions necessary?

When the Torah was given, the Shechinah descended for the sake of the Jewish people. (In a sense it was on hearing the Ten Commandments that they received the first *luchos*.) But this further revelation was for Moshe only and was due to his merit and prayers. Thus a greater degree of holiness was present in connection with the second *luchos*, and extra stringencies were required.

There was another reason Moshe had to ascend the mountain alone. The first *luchos* were given in public, amid thunder and lightning. This made them vulnerable to the influence of the evil eye, and consequently they

The Tablets 75

did not endure. Evidently even the miraculous *luchos* were not immune from the power of the evil eye! The second *luchos*, therefore, were given in a discreet manner, in an atmosphere of *tznius*, modesty. Moreover, sinning causes feelings of shame, and this creates a need for *tznius*.

The First and Second *Luchos*

We know that Moshe hewed the second *luchos*, whereas the first were entirely the work of God. But in some respects they were identical. The measurements were exactly the same, and both were made of sapphire and shaped with flames of fire.

How did they differ? The first *luchos* included every detail of the revealed and hidden Torah, whereas the second contained only the Ten Commandments.

But who wrote the second *luchos* — God or Moshe? The verse states, "And he was there with God forty days.... And he wrote upon the tablets the words of the covenant, the Ten Commandments." *Who* wrote is not immediately apparent. However, when we turn to the first verse of the chapter, we read, "God said to Moshe, 'Hew for yourself two tablets...and I will write upon the tablets.' " According to the *peshat*, the plain meaning of the text, it was God Who inscribed the second *luchos*, not Moshe. Like the first tablets, they were written with the finger of God.

However, the Midrash says that Moshe wrote the second *luchos*. But how can this be reconciled with the words of the verse, "I [God] will write"?

God had performed great miracles with the lettering of the first *luchos*; to reproduce these was impossible for Moshe. So God said to him, "I will grant you the power to inscribe these *luchos* just as I inscribed the first ones."

One commentator offers an interesting interpretation. Had the Jewish people not sinned by serving the golden calf, the first *luchos* would have remained intact. Then the nation would have been purified from every vestige of materialism. But due to that tragic error we have to toil hard and constantly strive for holiness and pure character traits. Great effort is also required in the area of Torah learning; only then does Heaven enable the student to derive the correct halachah, ruling.

The first *luchos* were formed and written by God. Moshe hewed the second *luchos* and also wrote out the letters in an ordinary manner. But the engraving involved a twofold miracle, and this was the work of God Himself. It is man's task to try to purify himself — this corresponds to the writing, which was the work of a human being. The engraving alludes to the Heavenly assistance that allows him to achieve his objective.

When the Torah was given, a covenant was formed between God and the Jewish people. Forty days later, due to that terrible idolatrous act, the *luchos* were shattered. This signaled the end of the covenant. It had become null and void. Moshe then ascended Mount Sinai with the second *luchos*, which symbolized the people's wish to renew the covenant. Finally, God inscribed the tablets with the Ten Commandments. The covenant had been restored.

Chapter Six
The Rock of Kadesh

For close to forty years Miriam accompanied the Jewish people in their wanderings through the desert. But while the nation was encamped in Kadesh, she passed away. Her demise had dramatic and far-reaching consequences.

The well of Miriam had provided the people with water, but with Miriam's death this source dried up. Desperately thirsty, throngs of people made their way toward Moshe and Aharon. The Midrash describes how the brothers reacted when they saw the crowds surging toward them.

"Why are they all gathering together?" Moshe asked Aharon.

"Aren't they the children of Avraham, Yitzchak, and Yaakov?" replied Aharon. "By nature and inheritance they are kindhearted people. Surely they've come to do kindness for our sister."

"You think they've come for a beneficial purpose, but that can't be true," Moshe said. "Had they come for Miriam's sake, the princes [the heads of the tribes] would be in the front, followed by the ordinary folk. But this is just a mass of people — there is no order among them."

And indeed, "The people quarreled with Moshe and

78 *Keystones of the World*

spoke, saying, 'If only we had died when our brothers died before God!' " (*Bemidbar* 20:3). Since Aharon loved peace, and spared no effort to promote harmony and goodwill within their ranks, they didn't have the temerity to argue with him.

"Better to have died of plague, like the generation of the spies," the people cried in their anguish, "for there is no worse death than that from thirst."

"And why have you brought up the assembly of God into this desert, so that we and our animals should die there? And why have you made us come up from Egypt, to bring us to this evil place...and there is no water to drink!" (ibid., 4–5).

In the face of this crisis, Moshe and Aharon turned away from the people and went to the entrance of the Tent of Meeting. There they fell on their faces, and God appeared to them.

> "God spoke to Moshe, saying, 'Take the staff and gather the congregation, you and Aharon, your brother, and you shall speak to the rock before their eyes; and it shall give forth its water, and you shall bring forth for them water from the rock, and you shall give the congregation and their animals to drink.'
>
> "Moshe took the staff from before God, as He commanded him. And Moshe and Aharon gathered the assembly before the rock, and he said to them, 'Listen now, you rebels, shall we bring forth water for you from this rock?'
>
> "Moshe lifted his hand, and with his staff he

The Rock of Kadesh   79

smote the rock twice; and the water came out in abundance, and the congregation drank and their animals.

"God said to Moshe and Aharon, 'Since you did not believe in Me, to sanctify Me before the eyes of the children of Israel, therefore you shall not bring this assembly into the land that I have given them.'

"These are the waters of Merivah, because the children of Israel quarreled with God, and He was sanctified through them" (*Bemidbar* 20:7–13).

What happened in this incident? What did Moshe and Aharon do wrong? Explanations abound on the topic, but for an overall picture we begin with the Midrashic interpretation.

In what was a supernatural occurrence, the entire nation stood next to the rock, though it was of no extraordinary size. This was to enable each person to witness the miracle. The space next to the rock in Kadesh was one of the places where החזיק מועט את המרובה, "the small contained the great." On another comparable occasion, all the people assembled at the entrance of the Tent of Meeting (see *Vayikra* 8:4).

Every generation has its mockers, and it was these people who began to foment trouble.

"You think there's going to be a miracle? Don't you know that Moshe was Yisro's shepherd? He's taken us to this rock because he knows it contains water — shepherds are very knowledgeable about these things. So let's choose the rock ourselves; let him bring out water from this other rock."

80   *Keystones of the World*

Moshe found himself in a quandary. If he listened to them, he would disobey God's command (he had been instructed to speak to a specific rock), and God "traps wise men with their cunning" (*Iyov* 5:13).

One commentator explains this verse from a different angle. Moshe was aware of a certain fact about his own destiny: he was predisposed to come to grief through water. He tried to prevent this from happening, but his attempt to do so boomeranged.

Thirty-nine years earlier, when the people were encamped in Refidim, Moshe was told to hit the rock and thus provide water for the nation. God instructed Moshe, "Pass on before the people and take with you of the Elders of Israel" (*Shemos* 17:5). Only the Elders and the righteous people were to witness his action. Why was it necessary to exclude the rest of the nation? The commentator explains that they might have criticized Moshe.

But this time Moshe intended to sanctify God's Name in front of the whole nation. Everyone would see water issue from the rock, and he was determined not to be caught by excluding potential troublemakers. But it was precisely this that trapped him. He was criticized, he did become annoyed, and this led to a severe punishment.

The Midrash continues its narrative. For forty years Moshe was very careful not to become irritated with the people, because he was afraid of the oath God had sworn: "Surely not one of these men in this evil generation shall see the good land which I swore to give to your fathers" (*Devarim* 1:35). Another verse says, "All those who pro-

The Rock of Kadesh

voke Me shall not see it" (*Bemidbar* 14:23). Included in this punishment was every person who angered God, not only those involved with the sin of the spies.

But now people kept saying to him, "Bring out water from this other rock!"

Then Moshe shouted, "Listen now, *morim*! Should I bring out water for you from *this* rock when I haven't been commanded to do so?"

What did Moshe have in mind when he called them *morim*? There are various interpretations: rebels, idiots, or those who teach their teachers. Alternatively, Moshe was comparing them to archers; he was hinting at their evil tongues, which let loose lethal missiles, as it is written, "Their tongue is a sharpened arrow" (*Yirmeyahu* 9:7).

"Moshe lifted his hand and struck the rock" (*Bemidbar* 20:11). He hit the rock God had chosen, and it began to drip water, as it says, הן הכה צור ויזובו מים, "Behold, he struck the rock and water emerged..." (*Tehillim* 78:20). The word הן seems superfluous, but it can also mean "one." He hit the rock *once*, and it merely dripped water.

This elicited the following response: "Son of Amram, is this water for nursing babies or for those being weaned from milk?"

Moshe grew annoyed and hit the rock again and again — "he struck the rock twice with the staff." Then water came pouring out in abundance and soaked all the people who had been complaining against Moshe and Aharon: "...and streams overflowed" (ibid.).

Moshe hit only the rock God had specified, but every rock and pebble in the vicinity gushed with water simultaneously, including the one chosen by the people.

82   *Keystones of the World*

What did Moshe do wrong? According to a different *midrash*, there were four transgressions.

First, "you did not believe in Me" (*Bemidbar* 20:12). The brothers had not been instructed to hit the rock, but Moshe did so nevertheless.

Second, "you did not sanctify Me" (*Devarim* 32:51). He should have agreed to use any rock they specified.

Third, "you trespassed against Me" (ibid.) by saying to the people, "Shall we bring forth water for you from *this* rock?" This question gave the impression that God did not have the power to make every rock produce water.

Finally, "you rebelled against My command" (*Bemidbar* 27:14). When God said, ודברתם אל הסלע, He meant, "You shall speak beside the rock." He expected Moshe and Aharon to learn a chapter of Torah beside the rock, after which water would flow from it. But this was not done.

"Because You Did Not Believe in Me..."

The Midrash asks, didn't Moshe commit a greater wrong than this? In *Bemidbar* ch. 11 we read of how the people were grumbling about the manna; they were tired of it, and they longed for meat. Consequently God told Moshe that He would provide them with meat for a whole month.

Moshe replied, "The people among whom I am are six hundred thousand men on foot.... If flocks and herds are slaughtered for them, will they suffice for them? Or if all the fish of the sea are gathered together for them, will

The Rock of Kadesh

they suffice for them?" God answered, "Is the hand of God grown short?" (*Bemidbar* 11:21–23).

Moshe's reply is interpreted in various ways, but the Midrash says it demonstrated a lack of faith — to a greater degree than on this later occasion. So why was he sentenced to death now and not then?

It is comparable to a king whose friend had behaved arrogantly toward him. The king didn't become angry. But when this man acted in the same way in front of the king's soldiers, the king sentenced him to death.

God said to Moshe, "On the first occasion, what you did was between Me and you, so I wasn't angry. But now that you have sinned in public, it is impossible to tolerate it." Thus the verse states, "Because you did not believe in Me, to sanctify Me *before the eyes of the children of Israel*, therefore you shall not bring this assembly into the land that I have given them" (*Bemidbar* 20:12).

On this same verse the Midrash brings another parable, which illustrates a different point.

Two women were being sentenced by the *beis din*. One was guilty of adultery, and the other had eaten unripe *shemittah* figs. (It is forbidden to eat *shemittah* fruit before it is ripe — see *Vayikra*, ch. 25.) The latter said to the judges, "Since I'm being punished together with her, people will say that I too am an adulteress! Please publicize exactly what I did wrong, and then they will know the truth."

They brought some unripe *shemittah* figs, and these were hung on her neck. Then they announced, "The other woman committed adultery and was punished, and she ate unripe *shemittah* figs and was punished."

84   *Keystones of the World*

In the same spirit, Moshe said to God, "You have decreed that I should die in the desert with the generation who left Egypt — a generation who aroused Your anger. In the future people will say that I am like them! Please let the reason for my punishment be recorded." The verse therefore states, "Because you did not believe in Me, to sanctify Me before the eyes of the children of Israel, therefore you shall not bring this assembly into the land...."

But what is the significance of the unripe *shemittah* figs? Why does the Midrash use this particular analogy? A commentator explains that the first woman was guilty of a sin that deserved the death penalty. So too the generation that left Egypt rebelled against God and was sentenced to die in the wilderness. The second woman consumed unripe *shemittah* figs, fruit which was not yet fit to be eaten and enjoyed. Likewise, through mishap and error, Moshe and Aharon failed to sanctify God's Name at the right moment, at the time intended by Divine Providence.

Why Was Aharon Blamed?

"God said to Moshe and Aharon, 'Because you did not believe in Me...you shall not bring this assembly into the land.' " Why was Aharon punished? Surely it was only Moshe who was at fault.

The Midrash tells us that Aharon was praised for his restraint in the face of this indictment. "And of Levi he [Moshe] said, 'Your *tumim* and Your *urim* belong to Your pious man [Aharon], whom You tried at Massah, with

The Rock of Kadesh

85

whom You strove at the waters of Merivah' " (*Devarim* 33:8). A commentator explains that God "contended" with Aharon and spoke as if he had sinned, blaming him as well as Moshe. But to his eternal credit, Aharon remained silent and accepted God's words. He did not try to justify himself.

But we are still left with the question, "Why was Aharon blamed?" According to a different *midrash*, the fact that Aharon was considered guilty teaches us a principle: one who is attached to a transgressor is considered like the transgressor.

Others say Aharon was punished because he failed to protest against Moshe's behavior; while Moshe hit the rock, Aharon merely looked on. A different commentator points out that God said, "And you shall speak to the rock," to both Moshe and Aharon. Neither obeyed, so both were blamed.

One commentator brings an interesting answer in connection with a *midrash*. The *midrash* quotes a verse from *Iyov*: "He [God] removes the speech [literally, 'the lip'] of the faithful and takes away the sense of the elders" (*Iyov* 12:20). Who are the faithful and the elders? Yitzchak, Yaakov, Aharon, and Moshe. It is written about Moshe, "He is faithful in all My house" (*Bemidbar* 12:7). And with regard to Aharon it says, "The law of truth was in his mouth" (*Malachi* 2:6); truth is equivalent to faithfulness. Since Moshe and Aharon sinned with their lips, saying, "Listen now, you rebels!" they were refused entry into the Land of Israel.

The commentator explains that in reality this decree had been ordained thirty-eight years earlier, at the time of the incident with the spies. Since that generation sinned grievously, they did not deserve to experience *techiyas hameisim*, resurrection. God therefore arranged to rectify this situation through Moshe and Aharon. The brothers had to forgo something vital and precious, and their loss would enable the generation of the spies to achieve *techiyas hameisim*. In line with the divine plan, Moshe lost control of his tongue and cried, "Listen now, you rebels!" This was the pretext for the punishment, and Aharon was included because he was with Moshe at the time.

But another commentator asserts that both Moshe and Aharon were truly guilty. In his view, none of the transgressions mentioned by the Rabbis in connection with the rock is serious enough to warrant such a severe punishment. Moreover, God metes out retribution measure for measure, and this decree doesn't seem to fit the sin. Why should Moshe be barred from the Land of Israel because he hit the rock or became angry? And why did Aharon suffer the same fate?

Moshe and Aharon had both committed a sin on an earlier occasion, but only now did God reveal the punishment they deserved. This can be illustrated through a parable. A boy behaved very badly toward his father, but the latter didn't react at all. He didn't want to embarrass his son, so he completely ignored the incident. Later the boy was caught in some trifling misdemeanor, and then the father gave him a thrashing.

Aharon was greatly at fault in making the golden calf. He certainly did not serve the calf, and his intentions in creating it were absolutely pure. The people were

The Rock of Kadesh

on the brink of idol worship, and by making the calf, Aharon meant to delay matters for a few hours. In the meantime Moshe would return, and no real harm would have been done. But matters developed otherwise. The people did serve the calf, and consequently thousands died, some by the sword and others from plague.

Since he had prevented so many people from entering the Land of Israel, it was decreed that he should suffer the same fate. But God didn't want to demean Aharon by punishing him together with these men, so He waited until the appropriate moment. When He commanded the brothers to speak to the rock, Moshe hit it, and it was this minor offense that triggered the pronouncement "You shall not bring this assembly into the land."

Moshe's major error was in connection with the spies. The people were eager to send spies to the Land of Israel, but they didn't have any detailed agenda in mind. They simply wanted the spies to bring back information about which route to take and which cities to conquer, as God had said to Moshe, "Send for yourself men, that they may spy out the land of Canaan" (*Bemidbar* 13:2).

But when he was briefing the spies, Moshe raised several points that God hadn't mentioned. "You shall see the land, what it is, and the people who live in it, whether they are strong or weak, few or many...and what cities they are that they live in, whether in camps or in strongholds" (ibid., 18–19). Moshe intended the spies to discover the answers to these questions; they would then inform the rest of the nation that the inhabitants were strong and the cities large and fortified. Consequently, Moshe thought, the people would fully appreciate God's

88   *Keystones of the World*

kindness in driving out such a formidable enemy.

This was his plan, but it was not to be. When the spies returned with their report, they dealt with Moshe's queries in a manner that terrified the people. Panic broke out among them, and they criticized Moshe, Aharon, and even God. As a result they were condemned to die in the desert, a fate that also befell Moshe because he had caused this tragic situation. And for the same reason as with Aharon, God delayed revealing his punishment until the incident with the rock.

The Well of Miriam

> And the people stayed in Kadesh, and Miriam died there and was buried there. And there was no water for the congregation....
>
> *(Bemidbar* 20:1–2)

The Sages of the Talmud tell us that the well was in Miriam's merit. When Moshe was hidden in the river as a baby, Miriam stood by and waited to see what would happen to her brother. As a reward the well of Miriam sustained the Jewish people for close to forty years.

When she died, there was a period when the nation was left without water. One commentator explains that the rock that would now provide water was none other than Miriam's well. This rock is given four names by the Torah:

1. עין משפט, as it says, "They returned and came to Ein Mishpat [the spring of judgment]; that is Kadesh" *(Bereishis* 14:7). It was so called because it would ultimately cause Moshe to be judged and punished.

The Rock of Kadesh

2. צור. When the nation was encamped in Refidim, God said to Moshe, "Behold, I will stand before you there upon the rock [הצור] in Chorev, and you shall strike the rock, and water shall emerge from it, that the people may drink" (*Shemos* 17:6). The appellation צור is sometimes used with reference to God, as in the verse "The Rock, His work is perfect" (*Devarim* 32:4), and on that occasion the Divine Presence appeared upon the rock.

3. סלע, as in our chapter: "And the people stayed in Kadesh.... And God spoke to Moshe, saying..., 'And you shall speak to the rock before their eyes, and it shall give forth its water.' " In Kadesh, the Divine Presence was not revealed, so the rock is merely referred to as הסלע. The well departed with Miriam's death and returned in Moshe and Aharon's merit. God therefore said to Moshe, "And you shall speak to *the* rock."

4. באר, as it is written, "This is the *well* about which God said to Moshe, 'Gather the people, and I will give them water' " (*Bemidbar* 21:16).

The Sages of the Talmud say that the manna, the protective Clouds of Glory, and the well were granted to the Jewish people in the merit of Moshe, Aharon, and Miriam respectively. With the death of Miriam the well returned in the merit of her brothers; and when Aharon passed away, the Clouds of Glory and the well existed only because of Moshe. Clearly Moshe alone was able to sustain all three blessings. So why was each one initially in the merit of Moshe, Aharon, and Miriam?

While Aharon and Miriam were alive, the burden of tending to the needs of the people was shared among the three siblings. Moshe was not solely responsible for the nation, and consequently his merit wasn't sufficient to provide all three blessings. When Miriam died, her brothers' duties increased, and the more they labored, the greater was their merit. Now they were able to sustain the well, too. Later, bereft of Aharon, Moshe was left as the sole shepherd of Israel; everything was placed squarely on his shoulders. Only then could he merit the manna, the well, and the Clouds of Glory.

But when Miriam died, the blessing of water was not automatically granted to her brothers. First they had to busy themselves with the needs of the people and take up Miriam's burden. God commanded, "Gather the congregation, you and Aharon, your brother, and [both of] you shall speak to the rock" (*Bemidbar* 20:8). Moreover, on this first occasion after Miriam's death, God wanted both brothers to be involved in providing water to inform the people that henceforth the well would be in the merit of Moshe and Aharon.

However, apart from assembling the nation, the brothers did not act together. Aharon didn't participate, Moshe alone dealt with the rock, and both were held guilty.

Another commentator explains that when Moshe and Aharon assembled the people, they clustered around Miriam's rock. Fully aware that they had received water in her merit, they now wanted Moshe and Aharon to continue to use the well of Miriam. According to their way of thinking, how could it be otherwise? This was the rock that had miraculously given water in the past. But Moshe had other considerations. Every tzaddik has a different *shoresh*, spiritual root, and Moshe chose another rock with the aim of opening a new source. This was the source that would provide water, not Miriam's rock.

He therefore entreated the people, שמעו נא **המרים** המן הסלע הזה נוציא לכם מים, "Please listen! You think I'm from the same *shoresh* as my sister, Miriam [*morim* implies *Miriam*], but this is not true. So do you want us to bring out water from that rock?"

Moshe then used the rock of his choice, an action that did not meet with God's approval. He should have acceded to the wishes of the Jewish people on this occasion.

The Purpose of the Staff

Why did God instruct Moshe to "take the staff...and speak to the rock" (*Bemidbar* 20:8)? What was the function of the staff?

All the signs and wonders Moshe performed in Egypt were done with a specific staff in his hand, as it says, "And you shall take in your hand this staff, with which you shall do the signs" (*Shemos* 4:17). God now told Moshe to "take *the* staff" and use it as a conduit for a further miracle.

Some say Moshe took the staff of Aharon from the Tent of Meeting. Aharon's staff had miraculously budded and blossomed and was kept as a reminder of Korach's fate when he rebelled against Moshe (see *Bemidbar* 17:23). In obedience to God's command, a piece of dry wood had flowered and in the process had provided the moisture necessary for growth. Now this same staff would bring forth water from a rock, in response to the divine command expressed by Moshe. But he failed to speak to the rock and struck it instead.

A *midrash* relates that the staff Moshe used was engraved on both sides. On one side was inscribed the divine Name that dries up water; this enabled Moshe to bring about the miracle at the Red Sea. On the other was the Name that does precisely the opposite, and he was about to employ the staff for this purpose. But when he became angry with the people, he accidentally hit the rock with the wrong side of the staff. Nothing happened. The second time he used the staff correctly, and water poured out from the rock.

The Value of Speech

Why was it so crucial to speak to the rock? What was the purpose of talking to an inanimate object?

Let us imagine that Moshe and Aharon had indeed spoken to the rock. The people would have seen the water gush forth in response to Moshe's words, and this would have stirred their hearts. "The rock doesn't speak, hear, or need any sustenance whatsoever, yet it immediately fulfills God's command. How much more so should we serve God with devotion and wholehearted obedience!"

A different opinion notes that on the earlier occasion in Refidim God had told Moshe to strike the rock and thus provide water for the people (*Shemos* 17:6). But

The Rock of Kadesh   93

the second time He commanded, "And you shall *speak* to the rock." This miracle was intended to inform the people in a vivid and memorable way that God's actions are not uniform and repetitive, but "new every morning" (*Eichah* 3:23).

What was the aim of the mitzvah regarding the rock? To arouse the nation to repentance, according to another commentator. The Jewish people had their doubts about Moshe's leadership; they resented the fact that he had brought them to this particularly barren part of the desert. They had a similar complaint against God, Who had plucked them from civilization and placed them in an uninhabited wasteland. God therefore planned a twofold miracle, a miracle that would change their thinking in both respects. It would illustrate clearly not only the greatness and kindness of the King, but also the goodness of His devoted servant, who acts on their behalf at the request of his Master.

The commentator explains that the miracles related in Tanach can be divided into three categories. The first type is the hidden miracle; for example, rain descended or people were saved from illness or sorrow. This kind of miracle can occur through the prayer of righteous individuals. Avraham prayed to God and Avimelech was healed; likewise, Moshe begged God to forgive the people for worshiping the calf, thereby saving them from utter destruction.

The second type is the open miracle. God would command one of His servants to perform a certain action or series of actions, and this was followed by the actual miracle. For example, God instructed Moshe, "Throw it

94 — Keystones of the World

[the staff] on the ground" (*Shemos* 4:3). Moshe obeyed and the staff turned into a snake.

The third type is the miracle that transcends nature; no action is required except speech, the speech of God's servants. Speaking is an intellectual act and of greater value than any other physical expression. Yehoshua performed a miracle of this kind when he said, "Sun, stand still in Givon, and, Moon, in the valley of Ayalon" (*Yehoshua* 10:12). It was a miracle of this type that would banish the nation's discontent and bring them to a true appreciation of God's greatness and benevolence.

God therefore commanded Moshe, "And you shall speak to the rock," adding, "And it shall give forth *its* water." God did not want the water to flow into the rock from another source, as on the first occasion in Refidim. Something more fundamental was about to happen. By speaking to the rock at God's behest, Moshe would change stone into water. Then the people would think, *True, God has brought us out of Egypt and into a wilderness, but what is the harm in that? He is constantly with us — He has the power to transform a desert into a pool of water! As long as He is here, everything is here.*

But how was Moshe's stature and kindness to be fully grasped by the nation?

This would be illustrated by the second type of miracle — an open miracle involving an action. Once the water was available, Moshe would direct it to each tribe with his staff, as God said to Moshe, "Take the staff...and you shall bring forth water for them."

However, Moshe and Aharon did not want to speak to the rock. They assumed that the people were too rebel-

The Rock of Kadesh

95

lious to be fit for a miracle of this kind and thought that God would "change His mind." Instead they decided to perform the second type of miracle, and Moshe hit the rock with his staff, as he had done in Refidim.

This only demonstrated the caliber of the servant, not the King, and God rebuked Moshe and Aharon. "You didn't believe in Me" (*Bemidbar* 20:12) — you didn't trust that I would do as I said. "You trespassed against Me" (*Devarim* 32:51) because you profaned My glory and failed to show the foolishness of their complaints. And "you rebelled against My command" (*Bemidbar* 20:24) by not adhering to My instructions.

Another commentator sees particular significance in the phrase, "And you shall speak to the rock *before their eyes.*" When the Torah was given, the people were on a very elevated spiritual level and were able to see what is normally only heard. As the verse relates (*Shemos* 20:15), "And all the people saw the sounds" that came forth from the Almighty. Now God wanted this generation to see the divine speech issue from the throat of Moshe and everyone would observe its effect on the rock. This taste of the revelation at Mount Sinai would strengthen the faith of the Jewish people and prepare them for the ceremony of the covenant on the plains of Moav (see *Devarim*, ch. 29). Upon seeing the rock react to the Godly speech, they would serve God humbly and do whatever He commanded.

It was essential, therefore, for the people to prepare their faculty of sight in order that their eyes should be ready to see God's speech, for this was no ordinary event, but one of great holiness. Thus God told Moshe,

ודברתם אל הסלע לעיניהם, "You shall speak to the rock before their eyes," implying that they should make the necessary preparations.

But the message was never delivered. In his anger with his flock, Moshe said, "Listen now, you rebels!" and he failed to pass on God's instructions. Consequently, when Moshe spoke to the rock, the divine speech had no effect, and he was forced to hit it instead. לא האמנתם בי, God accused Moshe; you failed to imbue the people with faith.

Another commentator also remarks on the use of the word לעיניהם, "before their eyes." One would think that באזניהם, "in their hearing," would be more appropriate. But לעיניהם indicates understanding and knowledge. Similarly, when Adam and Chavah ate the forbidden fruit (see *Bereishis* 3:6–7), "the eyes of both of them were opened" to knowledge of good and evil. God wanted the Jewish people to understand the value of divine speech, and it was for this reason that He commanded Moshe to speak to the rock.

Why on both occasions (in Refidim and in Kadesh) did God quench the nation's thirst by means of a rock? Why, for example, did He not bring down quantities of rain?

God wanted to convey an important lesson. The heart of man is compared to a stone, on which it is hard to engrave the words of the Torah. How can man possibly overcome the promptings of his heart, which draw him toward evil? Through the help of Heaven, the heart can change its nature and turn toward Torah and mitzvos. It is God's power that can draw water from a hard rock and

The Rock of Kadesh

transform man's heart into a surging spring.

But there is no denying that the initial stages are difficult. And God hinted at the condition of the people when He commanded Moshe to hit the rock on that first occasion in Refidim, for then their hearts were still of stone. But at the end of almost forty years, Moshe was told to *speak* to the rock, because this new generation possessed hearts of flesh; the Jewish people were now fulfilling the mitzvos quite naturally and willingly. It was to this generation that Moshe said, "And you who cleave to Hashem your God are alive, every one of you this day" (*Devarim* 4:4), and it was these people who later entered the Land of Israel.

However, when they started quarreling in Kadesh, Moshe mistakenly thought that their hearts were still made of stone, and he deemed it appropriate to strike the rock, as he had done in Refidim. That was the cause of his fateful error.

Clearly many opinions agree that Moshe's sin was to strike rather than to speak, and it is in connection with this action that one commentator asks an obvious question. Why does the verse state, "Moshe raised his hand and struck the rock"? Obviously he had to lift his hand. Similarly, the verse says about Avraham, "And Avraham stretched out his hand and took the knife to slaughter his son" (*Bereishis* 22:10).

We know that the 248 limbs of man correspond to the 248 positive commandments; each limb is assigned a specific mitzvah. Moreover, holy and righteous people have purified their bodies to the extent that every limb is ready and eager to perform the mitzvah of its own accord.

Avraham was one such person. So when he came to bind his son, there was no reluctance whatsoever on the part of his limbs to carry out this task. But as he prepared to actually slaughter Yitzchak, he noticed that his hand was unwilling to cooperate. He had to force himself to carry out this act: "And Avraham stretched out his hand and took the knife." Then the angel called out, "Avraham, Avraham!... Don't stretch out your hand to the lad, and don't do anything to him" (ibid. 11–12).

Moshe found himself in a similar predicament. When he hit the rock in Refidim, his hand acted of its own volition, since he was fulfilling God's command. But on this occasion, when he was instructed to speak to the rock, he had to expend real effort in lifting his hand, because this action was against God's will.

The Livestock

God instructed Moshe to "give the congregation and their animals to drink" from the water that would issue from the rock. Why does the Torah mention the animals?

As one commentator points out, they are referred to three times in this episode. This conveys the fact that an abundance of water issued from the rock; it was enough not only for the whole nation, but also for their beasts.

According to the Midrash, the divine command to water the animals teaches us that God cares about the property of the Jewish people. One commentator offers an interesting insight into the Torah's attitude toward animals. It is written, "And His mercies are on all His

The Rock of Kadesh 99

works" (*Tehillim* 145:9), and "He gives nourishment to all flesh" (ibid. 136:25). Nevertheless, God does not alter the course of nature for the sake of animals. The Jewish people were miraculously provided with water from the rock, and there was even enough for the beasts, but only because "God cares about the property of Israel." Just as He had pity on the people themselves, He likewise had pity on their possessions.

The Sages of the Talmud say that it is forbidden for a man to eat before he has fed his animals. However, with regard to drinking, human beings take priority, as is proved by Rivkah's behavior toward Eliezer. First she said, "Drink, my master," and only then did she water the camels (*Bereishis* 24:18–19). One can bring a further proof from God's words to Moshe on this occasion: "And you shall give the congregation and [then] their animals to drink."

One commentator provides a beautiful explanation on this verse. God commanded Moshe, והשקית את העדה ואת בעירם, "You shall give the congregation and their animals to drink." Finally, after all the altercation and upset, the verse says, ותשת העדה ובעירם, "The congregation drank and their animals." But the words העדה, the congregation, and בעירם, their animals, are no longer separated by the conjunction את. Why?

When God willingly and wholeheartedly bestows a blessing on His people, it is invariably of the finest quality. Quality is the supreme attribute; quantity is considered a secondary manifestation of the divine will. God said to the Jewish nation, "You shall eat your bread to satisfaction" (*Vayikra* 26:5), meaning that eating only a small amount would satisfy their hunger. This promised an exalted way of life, and the Talmudic Sages say that the people were not content until they heard these words.

As for the manna, the "bread of the mighty," which came straight from God, this was a spiritual food and a source of spiritual delight. Naturally it excelled in quality, not quantity; however much manna a person gathered, he never had more than an *omer*, the prescribed measure, for each member of his family, and that was always sufficient.

Drinking can also be an elevated act, and of course this is something that is totally beyond an animal. A beast drinks in order to still the thirst in his belly. The water in Kadesh could have been as sublime as the manna, but everything went awry when Moshe and Aharon failed to follow God's instructions. Had they only obeyed God and sanctified His Name, the water, and consequently the drinking, would have been of the highest spiritual quality. We can see this was what God intended, for the word את in the earlier verse divides the people from the animals.

God had commanded Moshe, "You shall bring out water for them," but in the end, it gushed forth in large quantities — "And the water came out in abundance." The quality was lacking, and the people drank much as the animals drank. The concluding verse therefore omits the word את and states ותשת העדה ובעירם.

The Rock of Kadesh   *101*

The Nature of the Sin —
Other Explanations in Brief

- When the people demanded water, Moshe and Aharon fell on their faces before God and entreated His help. But they were fully capable of acting on their own initiative. Yehoshua held back the sun and moon, and Eliyahu brought down fire from Heaven; likewise, Moshe and Aharon could have provided water for the nation. Since this was an emergency, they shouldn't have delayed matters for an instant. Had Moshe acted like his successor, he would have brought about a great *kiddush Hashem* (sanctification of God's Name), for the people would have seen that God changes nature in order to fulfill the decree of His servant.

- The Sages of the Talmud say that Moshe slighted the honor of the Jewish people when he said, "Listen now, you rebels!" We learn from this that one who slights the honor of the public is considered to have profaned the Name of God.

- Moshe used the word *morim*, rebels, because he was angry, and it was this response that aroused God's disapproval. It was not fitting for a great person like Moshe to be angry in front of the people, under these circumstances. They asked for water because they were extremely thirsty, so it was wrong of him to act in this manner. And when a man of Moshe's stature makes an error, it causes a *chillul Hashem* (profanation of God's Name), because the people learn from his every action and word. In this case they assumed that God must be

102   *Keystones of the World*

angry with them for requesting water, but they were mistaken.

- In Refidim the Divine Presence appeared on the rock, but on this occasion it did not. So when Moshe said, "Shall we bring out water for you from this rock?" rather than "shall *He*," it led to a misunderstanding. Some people thought that the water emerged through the brothers' skill and wisdom rather than by God's direct intervention. God therefore said, לא האמנתם בי, you didn't instill faith within their hearts.

- God said, ודברתם אל הסלע, and accordingly Moshe hit the rock. Here he was not at fault, because in this instance ודברתם means "you shall strike," not "you shall speak," as in the verse ותדבר את כל זרע הממלכה, "And she [*Atalyah*] smote all the royal issue" (*Divrei HaYamim* II 22:10). But he was punished for saying, "Shall *we* bring forth water" rather than "Shall *He* bring forth water."

The Waters of Strife

The Torah concludes the incident with the verse

> These are the waters of Merivah, because the children of Israel quarreled with God, and He was sanctified through them [the waters].
>
> (*Bemidbar* 20:13)

Why does the Torah state, "*These* are the waters of Merivah"? When Pharaoh decreed that all male children should be thrown into the river, he had a reason for choosing this death rather than any other. His astrolo-

The Rock of Kadesh   103

gers had informed him that the savior of Israel would be punished through water, and they assumed that he was destined to drown. But the Torah says, "*These* are the waters...." It was these waters, at Kadesh, which brought about Moshe's death, not the waters of the Nile.

The earlier verses make no mention of the people arguing with Hashem, yet here it is written, "because the children of Israel quarreled with God." Why were they accused of this sin? The Talmud says that it is from this verse that we derive the principle "He who quarrels with his teacher is considered to have quarreled with the Divine Presence."

The verse continues, "He was sanctified through them [the waters]." This statement is rather puzzling. How could God's Name be sanctified through this disastrous episode? On the contrary, in the preceding sentence we read, "Because you did not believe in Me, to sanctify Me...."

One commentator explains that it was only later that God's Name was sanctified through water. In the valleys of Arnon, God showed the Jewish nation that these were no ordinary waters; in defiance of natural law, they were rising higher than their source. The people referred to this miracle when they sang their song of praise to God: "...and from the valley to the high place" (*Bemidbar* 21:19).

But another commentator gives an entirely different interpretation. Moshe and Aharon died on account of these waters, and it was this tragedy that sanctified God's Name. It is written, "I will be sanctified through those who are close to Me" (*Vayikra* 10:3). When God executes justice upon holy people such as Moshe and Aharon, this makes a profound impression on the Jewish people, and they are thereby brought to fear of God.

"...and He was sanctified through them." The incident that is the epitome of strife nevertheless ends with holiness.

Chapter Seven
The Inscription on the Stones

Under the leadership of Yehoshua, the Jewish people crossed the River Jordan, which miraculously split before them. At last they entered the land promised to the Patriarchs. Twelve stones were lifted from the river, taken to Mount Eival, and built into an altar. The Torah was written on these stones, not only in Hebrew but in all seventy languages, so that every nation could read it. Finally they were carried to Gilgal and set up there as a memorial to the miracle God performed with the waters of the Jordan.

The twelve stones, therefore, played a dual role. First, they were inscribed with the words of the Torah. This commandment was of great significance for the Jewish and gentile nations. Second, they served as a memorial to the miracle at the Jordan, a reminder of the omnipotence of the Creator.

Part One — The Stones in the Jordan

We begin with *sefer Yehoshua*, chapter 3, in which Yehoshua addresses the people and prepares them for the imminent miracle.

Yehoshua said, "By this you shall know that the

106 *Keystones of the World*

Living God is in your midst and that He will without fail drive out from before you the Canaanites, the Hittites.... Behold, the Ark of the Covenant of the Master of all the earth passes on before you in the Jordan. And now take for yourselves twelve men from the tribes of Israel, a man for every tribe. And it shall come to pass, that as the soles of the feet of the priests, bearers of the Ark of God, Master of all the earth, shall rest in the waters of the Jordan, the waters of the Jordan will be cut off, the waters that come down from above, and they will stand as one column."

(*Yehoshua* 3:10–13)

Once the nation had crossed over, it was time for the stones to be lifted from the river. The waters had not yet resumed their natural course, and the *kohanim* were still standing on dry land in the Jordan, together with the stone tablets that were contained in the Ark:

1. And it was when the entire nation had completed crossing the Jordan, God said to Yehoshua, 2. "Take for yourselves twelve men from the people, a man from every tribe, 3. and command them, saying, 'Lift from here, from the Jordan, from the place where the priests' feet are standing firmly, twelve stones and carry them across with you and set them in the lodging place where you will lodge this evening.' "

4. Yehoshua summoned the twelve men whom he had prepared from the children of Israel, a man from every tribe. 5. And Yehoshua said to them,

The Inscription on the Stones 107

"Pass before the Ark of Hashem your God into the Jordan. Raise every man one stone upon his shoulder, according to the number of tribes of the children of Israel, 6. so that this will be a sign among you. For in the future, when your children will ask, saying, 'What is the meaning of these stones for you?' 7. you shall tell them, 'That the waters of the Jordan were cut off before the Ark of the Covenant of God; when it passed by the Jordan, the waters of the Jordan were cut off.' And these stones shall be a memorial for the children of Israel forever."

8. And so the children of Israel did just as Yehoshua commanded and lifted twelve stones from the Jordan, as God had told Yehoshua, according to the number of the tribes of the children of Israel, and carried them to the place where they lodged and placed them there.

9. And Yehoshua erected twelve stones in the Jordan, in the place where the feet of the priests, bearers of the Ark of the Covenant, were standing. They are there to this day.

(Yehoshua 4:1–9)

The Selection of the Twelve Men

In chapter 3, before the Jordan parted, we read that Yehoshua ordered the selection of twelve men, one from each tribe. But surprisingly, only in chapter 4 do we read of God's command to Yehoshua to choose twelve men for the task of lifting the stones. How could Yehoshua have acted before being instructed?

Of course, the command was given before the action. As illustrated in the quoted text, the *mesorah* inserts a gap in the opening verse of chapter 4, between "And it was when the entire nation had completed crossing the Jordan" and "God said to Yehoshua." This is meant to indicate that the text following this gap, the detailed instructions to Yehoshua, were actually commanded earlier. Their placement here is a form of flashback, to indicate that the time had come for them to be put it into practice. (The actual narrative runs on from the first section of verse 1 straight on to verse 4, "Yehoshua summoned the twelve men.")

Twelve men, one from each tribe, were appointed to lift the twelve stones to signify that the whole of the nation crossed the Jordan. They had been chosen and were prepared — but for what purpose? They remained in ignorance of the nature of their mission until the people had reached the other side of the river. Only then did Yehoshua call on these men and issue instructions: "Pass before the Ark of God.... Raise every man one stone on his shoulder...."

However, others say there is no displacement of the text, and the verses are in chronological order. Only after the people had crossed the river did God speak to Yehoshua, and he immediately carried out the divine command.

That being so, we revert to the question, how could Yehoshua order the selection of twelve men before God had spoken to him?

The twelve men mentioned in chapter 3 were chosen of Yehoshua's own initiative for a different purpose.

The Inscription on the Stones

They were told to stand next to the Ark and witness the miracle on the spot. They were the ones who saw quite clearly that as soon as the feet of the *kohanim* touched the water, the river parted. These men could testify to the power of the Ark — the power of the Torah (for the Ark contained the stone tablets on which the Torah was written).

The difference in wording between the two relevant verses lends weight to this latter view. In verse 3:12, Yehoshua says, קחו לכם שני עשר איש משבטי ישראל איש אחד איש אחד **לשבט**, "Take for yourselves twelve men from the tribes of Israel, a man *for* every tribe." The word לשבט indicates that each man should represent his tribe. Naturally this task fell to the *nasi*, the prince of the tribe, who was chosen by virtue of his position. When the twelve *nesi'im* stood next to the Ark, it was as if the entire nation was present in that place, witnessing the miracle. The usage of איש, man, rather than אנשים, men, signifies that they were all of equal caliber — every one a *nasi* and an outstanding person.

By contrast, in verse 4:2, God tells Yehoshua, "Take for yourselves twelve men *from the people*, a man *from* every tribe [משבט]." They did not need to be *nesi'im*, but each one must be from a different tribe. When Yehoshua heard God's instructions, his thoughts turned to the *nesi'im* "whom he had prepared" for the task of being witnesses. Surely they could also accomplish this second mission, that of lifting the stones from the Jordan. This did not conflict with God's injunction that each man should be from a different tribe.

110   *Keystones of the World*

The Twelve Men Carry Out Their Task

How were matters arranged with the twelve men when the nation crossed the Jordan? Were they held back and told to wait until everyone else had reached the other side? Or did they cross with the rest of the people and then return to fetch the stones?

Again, opinion is divided. Some say that they emerged from the river and then went back for the stones (and this inevitably follows if God spoke to Yehoshua after the people had crossed over). The verse says, "And it was when the *entire* [*kol*] nation had completed crossing the Jordan" — this means that everybody crossed, including the twelve men.

A commentator explains that when Yehoshua conveyed God's words to the people, they did not respond eagerly and willingly. They were full of doubts and misgivings. "This is a very difficult mitzvah you're asking of us," they said. "Twelve men have to go back into the Jordan, and then start digging around each stone in order to dislodge it, which is bound to take some time. Meanwhile, they'll constantly be afraid that the waters will rush back to drown them. And how can they carry such heavy stones on their shoulders?"

When Yehoshua saw how hesitant they were, he called to the twelve men whom he had commanded to stand next to the Ark. They had seen the waters dry up under the feet of the *kohanim* and would therefore be the most confident under such circumstances. Yehoshua told them, "Pass before the Ark of God" (*Yehoshua* 4:5). He pointed out that they themselves had seen what the

The Inscription on the Stones

Ark had done, so there was no need to worry. Furthermore, these stones had already been prepared by God; therefore no digging would be necessary — they could be lifted easily from the riverbed.

But others say that the twelve men stayed behind on the eastern side of the Jordan with Yehoshua and awaited his command. The use of the word *kol*, usually translated as "all," doesn't prove that the entire people crossed the river, because this can also denote the majority.

First Yehoshua ordered the people to cross. With their leader behind them, they would feel confident that the waters wouldn't come rushing back. Then he addressed the twelve men who had remained with him, explaining that they were to lift the stones from the river and carry them to the other side.

According to either interpretation, the twelve men entered the Jordan separately from the rest of the people, and each one picked up a heavy stone unaided ("every man one stone upon his shoulder"). This was intended to make a memorable and lasting impression on the minds of the spectators and their descendants.

The phrase "lift from *here*" signifies that Yehoshua pointed to the stones that were lying in readiness beneath the feet of the *kohanim*. The *kohanim* raised their feet, and the twelve men lifted the stones, "every man one...upon his shoulder." Yehoshua thus indicated that the stones should be large, rather than of a size they would be able to carry easily in their hands.

The Monument in Gilgal

The stones were then carried to Mount Eival and built into an altar upon which the Torah was inscribed. Later on the same day, the altar was dismantled and taken to Gilgal, the site where the nation camped for the night (this is the "lodging place" mentioned in verse 4:3). These stones were formed into a monument that would last for many generations. Since the Jewish people were to stay in Gilgal for fourteen years, this was considered a suitable location for the memorial.

We know that the monument in Gilgal was still in existence after the destruction of the second Temple, because the Talmud says that certain *Tannaim* examined the stones and assessed the volume of each one to be forty *se'ah*. The location of the monument is marked on a mosaic map of the Land of Israel discovered in Medeba (now a town in Jordan). This map was composed about sixteen hundred years ago, and more than four centuries after the destruction of the Temple tourists still used to visit the site of the monument.

The twelve-stone monument in Gilgal erected by Joshua, as depicted in the ancient Medeba mosaic map.

The Inscription on the Stones   *113*

Incidentally, the figure of forty *se'ah* is useful as a basis for reckoning the volume of the cluster of grapes carried by the spies. The calculation runs as follows. As mentioned earlier, each man picked up a stone unaided and placed it on his shoulder. We also know that a load a person can lift onto his shoulder by himself is only one-third of the load he can carry if people help him to raise it. This means he is capable of carrying at least 120 *se'ah*.

Now we come to the cluster. The commentators explain that it took eight people to carry this enormous bunch of grapes, even though they helped each other (this is derived from the relevant verse in *Shelach* — *Bemidbar* 13:23). Since eight people were needed to bear the cluster, its volume was at least 960 *se'ah*.

A Sign and a Memorial

Yehoshua explained that the stones would act as a "sign" and a "memorial" (*Yehoshua* 4:6–7). What is the meaning behind these two expressions, which seem synonymous in this context?

The generation who experienced the miracle had no need of a memorial; it was hardly something they were likely to forget. But the stones were necessary as a sign. The people might imagine that the miracle was due to their own merit and power, and the stones were there to counteract this tendency. They were removed from under the feet of the bearers of the Ark — a sign that the Jordan parted through the power of the Ark and the holiness of the tablets.

Naturally the children of that era will ask, "What is

the meaning of these stones for you?" (*Yehoshua* 4:6). Why do you, who saw the miracle with your own eyes, need a memorial? Their parents will reply, "They are sign that 'the waters of the Jordan were cut off,' not before us, not due to our merit, but 'before the Ark of the covenant of God.' " Thus the "memorial" was for future generations.

The Stones Yehoshua Erected in the Jordan

We read that Yehoshua put an additional twelve stones in the Jordan (*Yehoshua* 4:9). These were separate from the other twelve, and for this reason the verse refers to them as "stones" rather than "*the* stones." Yehoshua was following in the footsteps of Moshe, his teacher, who built twelve pillars under Mount Sinai, corresponding to the twelve tribes of Israel.

The verse does not say that he was instructed to do this, but it is understood that here, too, he was fulfilling God's command. But according to a different commentator, this was something Yehoshua did on his own initiative.

What was the purpose of the second set of stones?

Once the first twelve had been removed, another set was put in exactly the same place, underneath the feet of the *kohanim*, to prevent them from sinking in the mud. The stones remained there, and these were also intended as a memorial to the miracle.

However, another opinion states that the stones were placed in the river before it parted. They clearly marked the area in which the water would stand in one

The Inscription on the Stones

115

column, and this tangible precursor to the miracle prepared the people for the actual event.

But another commentator explains that these stones were placed in the river after the *kohanim* had emerged from it. The first stones were taken from the spot where the *kohanim* were actually standing — ממצב רגלי הכהנים. But the second set was put there after they had left, *in place of* the spot they had occupied — hence the phrase תחת מצב רגלי הכהנים. Like the stones in Gilgal, they were made into a monument. The word הקים, literally, "he made rise," denotes that they were placed on top of each other and rose up out of the water as a memorial to the miracle.

The monument in the Jordan acted as a reinforcement to its counterpart in Gilgal. When the people would see twelve stones in two different places, they would understand that they corresponded to each other. Consequently the miracle was certain to be remembered even after a long period of time.

Yehoshua himself erected the stones in the Jordan and in Gilgal, in order to prove a point. The twelve great men could conceivably have felt slighted by the request to carry heavy stones, a task that required much physical effort. But any thoughts of this kind were soon dispelled when the leader himself started lifting the stones.

The stones remained in the Jordan "until this day." This means that they were still there at the time *sefer Yehoshua* was written. Alternatively, since people reading this phrase will apply it to their own time, it simply means "forever."

The Two Miracles

Chapter 4 ends with the following verses:

> He spoke to the children of Israel saying, "In the future, when your children ask their fathers, saying, 'What are these stones?' you shall inform your children, saying, 'On dry land Israel crossed this Jordan.' For Hashem your God dried up the waters of the Jordan before you until you crossed, as Hashem your God did to the Red Sea, which He dried up before us until we crossed. So that all the peoples of the earth would know the hand of God, that it is mighty, so that you will fear Hashem your God all the days."
>
> *(Yehoshua* 4:21–24)

In these verses Yehoshua refers to two miracles — the splitting of the Jordan and the splitting of the Red Sea. But he emphasizes that the same power, "Hashem your God," was the force behind both. The heathen warriors and conquerors of that time used to set up monuments on which were inscribed details of their exploits and victories. But Yehoshua makes it quite clear that this monument does not stem from a desire for self-glorification. On the contrary, it is a memorial to the deed of God: "And you shall inform your children...for Hashem your God dried up the waters of the Jordan."

Of course, most of this generation had not witnessed the splitting of the Red Sea. The exceptions were those who were under the age of twenty at the time of the fateful episode with the spies, and Yehoshua, Kalev, and the elders of the tribe of Levi. When referring to this miracle, therefore, Yehoshua speaks of God drying up the Red Sea "before us until we crossed," but he uses the second person in connection with the Jordan — "before *you* until *you* crossed."

Both miracles were for two purposes. First, "so that all the peoples of the earth would know the hand of God, that it is mighty." The plagues in Egypt and the miraculous parting of the Red Sea conveyed a clear message to the Egyptians that they ultimately could not ignore: God is *the* God and the Jewish nation, His people. The splitting of the Jordan was a display of strength intended for the nations living in Canaan who hadn't seen the miracle at the Red Sea; they would now be too terrified to interfere with the Jews for fear of incurring God's wrath. And the next verse (chapter 5) tells us that this was exactly what happened: "It was when all the Emorite...and all the Canaanite kings...heard that God had dried up the waters of the Jordan before the children of Israel until they had crossed, their hearts melted, and there was no longer spirit within them because of the children of Israel."

The second aim was to instill fear and faith into the hearts of the Jewish people, as it says after the splitting of the Red Sea, "And the people feared God, and they believed in God" (*Shemos* 14:31). The fear He intended to inspire was not merely dread of punishment, but fear of an exalted nature that is akin to awe — *yiras haromemus*.

There is an interesting *midrash* about Yaakov that provides an additional reason for the miracle at the Jordan. The Midrash quotes three different verses, from Torah, the Prophets, and the Writings, which hint that the river split before the Jewish nation in the merit of their forefather Yaakov.

In the Torah it is written, "With my stick I crossed this Jordan" (*Bereishis* 32:10). Yaakov placed his stick in the river and it parted.

In the Prophets it is written, "In dry land Israel crossed this Jordan" (*Yehoshua* 4:22). "Israel" refers to Yaakov, in whose merit this miracle occurred.

In the Writings it is written, "What ails you, Sea, that you flee; you, Jordan, that you turn backwards...at the Presence of the God of Yaakov" (*Tehillim* 114:5–7). This is an allusion to the splitting of the Jordan, in connection with which neither Avraham nor Yitzchak are mentioned — only Yaakov.

When the Jewish people stood at the banks of the Jordan, they were not worthy of a miracle on this scale. Their farseeing ancestor paved the way for his descendants by placing his stick in the River Jordan. Once the waters had parted for him, they could later part once more in his merit.

The splitting of the Jordan was unnecessary from a practical point of view. The spies crossed this river in a natural manner, as did King David when he was fleeing from Avshalom. But one purpose was to remind Yaakov's children about the merit of the "elect of the Patriarchs" — the miracle strengthened their faith in the God of Yaakov.

❁   ❁   ❁

The Inscription on the Stones   *119*

Part Two — The Writing on the Stones

Once the stones had been lifted out of the river, they were the focus of much activity before they were finally erected in Gilgal. To fill in the gap, we turn first to the *sidrah* of *Ki Savo* (*Devarim*, ch. 27). In *Ki Savo*, Moshe issues instructions to the people that were to be carried out after his passing.

> Moshe and the Elders of Israel commanded the people, saying, "Keep all the commandment which I command you this day. And it shall be on the day when you shall cross over the Jordan to the land that Hashem your God gives you that you shall erect for yourself large stones and coat them with lime. And you shall write upon them all the words of this law, when you have crossed over, in order that you may go into the land that Hashem your God gives you, a land flowing with milk and honey, as Hashem, the God of your fathers, has promised you.
>
> "And it shall be, when you have crossed over the Jordan, that you shall erect these stones, which I command you this day, on Mount Eival, and you shall coat them with lime. And there you shall build an altar to Hashem, your God, an altar of stones; you shall lift up no iron tool on them. You shall build the altar of Hashem your God of unhewn stones, and you shall offer burnt offerings on it to Hashem your God. And you shall sacrifice peace offerings and eat there; and you shall rejoice before Hashem your God. And you shall write upon

120   *Keystones of the World*

the stones all the words of this Torah; explain [them] well."...

Moshe commanded the people the same day, saying: "These shall stand on Mount Gerizim to bless the people...and these shall stand on Mount Eival for the curse...."

(Devarim 27:1–13)

Allusions to the merits of the Patriarchs are contained within these verses. The stones themselves hint at Yaakov, who is referred to as the "stone of Israel," the foundation stone of the Jewish nation. The burnt offerings are a reference to Yitzchak, who was willing to be bound and sacrificed to God. The building of an altar at Mount Eival parallels Avraham's construction on that site, as it says (*Bereishis* 12:6), "Avram passed into the land as far as the place of Shechem, until the plains of Moreh...and he built an altar there" (Mount Eival is next to the plains of Moreh).

Moshe and the Elders instructed the people to שמור את כל המצוה, "keep all the commandment." What does this mean? Were they referring to the whole Torah or one particular mitzvah?

It can be understood as an exhortation to the Jewish nation to observe every commandment. But according to another opinion they were referring only to the mitzvah of the stones, which they then went on to explain at length. The word שמור, keep, in this context means "remember," as in the verse about Yaakov and Yosef: "And his father remembered [שמר] the matter" (*Bereishis* 37:11). Since this commandment involved many details, they urged the

The Inscription on the Stones   *121*

people to remember them all.

Moshe would not be present when the time arrived for the mitzvah to be put into practice, and with this in mind he joined forces with the Elders in explaining it to the nation. In the future the Elders would be able to encourage the people to carry out their task by reminding them, "Moshe himself made us his partners when it came to this commandment."

The Link with the Land

> And you shall write upon them all the words of this Torah...in order [למען] that you may go into the land.
>
> (*Devarim* 27:3)

It is highly significant that this commandment was performed upon their entry into the Land of Israel.

On an earlier occasion Moshe said to the people, "Don't imagine that you are going to inherit the Land of Israel because you deserve it. The Canaanite nations are corrupt and evil, and that's why God is expelling them from the land. Furthermore, God intends to fulfill the promise He made to the Patriarchs."

But by performing the mitzvah with the stones, the Jewish nation did ultimately earn the land through their own merit.

Another commentator points out that the people needed strength — spiritual strength — to conquer the land. Writing the Torah on the stones helped them to remember and keep all the commandments, and this provided them with the necessary "muscle" with which to defeat the enemy.

Keystones of the World

Alternatively, למען can be translated as "because" rather than "in order."

It was only in the merit of the Torah that the people inherited the land, so they were commanded to write it down *because* they had entered the country.

Another commentator explains that the Land of Israel is only a means to an end, the end being the fulfilment of the precepts of the Torah. It was vital for the nation to understand the supremacy of Torah, and there were many pointers to this basic truth:

- When they crossed the Jordan, it was the Ark, the symbol of Torah, which was placed there first. The Ark caused the waters to part and remained in the river until the nation had reached the other side. With the splitting of the Jordan, the Jewish people in effect began to take possession of the land — the nations of Canaan were terrified by the miracle and ceased to be a serious obstacle. Clearly the existence of the Jews in this land was entirely dependent on Torah.

- As soon as they arrived they traveled to Mount Eival and wrote the Torah on the stones, because this was the very purpose for which the land was given — that they should occupy themselves with Torah within its borders.

- The country was rich in natural resources, "a land flowing with milk and honey, as Hashem, the God of your fathers has promised you" (*Devarim* 27:3). Why are the Patriarchs mentioned here? And why the seemingly unnecessary use of the word *you*?

The Inscription on the Stones 123

In *parashas Shemos* (3:8), God gave His initial promise for a land flowing with milk and honey. On previous occasions it was the Patriarchs to whom He spoke about the land, and there is no mention of milk and honey. But in *Shemos* He was talking to Moshe, the nation's representative. God never described the Land of Israel to the Patriarchs in these terms, because it was only their descendants who were given the Torah. The bounty of the land isn't intended to be enjoyed for its own sake, but is a conduit for serving God and fulfilling His Torah.

- A further indication of the centrality of Torah is apparent from the command to erect the stones at Mount Eival. As mentioned earlier, this was the very site where Avraham built an altar, on the occasion God first told him, "To your seed I will give this land" (*Bereishis* 12:7). In this significant place the Jewish people built an altar on which were inscribed the words of the Torah. The commandment was a clear sign that the gift of the land is dependent on the Torah.

One commentator attributes the timing of this mitzvah to the commandments dependent on the land. There are many mitzvos that are applicable only in the Land of Israel, and the writing on the stones refreshed the people's memories and enabled them to put the theory into practice.

Finally, an interesting analogy: just as we are commanded to affix mezuzos on our doors and gates, so the Jewish people were instructed to write the Torah on the stones when they entered the land.

124   *Keystones of the World*

The Writing, the Lime, and the Message
to the Nations

> And it shall be on the day when you shall cross over the Jordan...that you shall erect for yourselves large stones and coat them with lime. And you shall write upon them all the words of this law.
>
> (*Devarim* 27:2–3)

We know that the Torah was written on the stones in seventy languages to enable all the nations to read it. But why did God want them to read the Torah?

A commentator on the Talmud explains that God did not want the nations to be able to claim on the Day of Judgment, "We couldn't learn the Torah because we didn't have access to it."

The *Tannaim* Rabbi Yehudah and Rabbi Shimon hold differing opinions on the subject of the lime. Rabbi Yehudah says they wrote the Torah on the stones of the altar and then limed them. But if that was the case, how could the nations read words that were covered with lime? God placed within the heart of every people and kingdom *binah yeseirah*, additional perception and understanding. They intuitively knew exactly what had happened and realized that underneath the lime were the words of the Torah. Each nation's scribes came to the altar, scraped off the lime, copied down the Torah, and took the results of their labor back to their people. The gentiles thus had the opportunity to study the Torah and internalize its principles.

However, Rabbi Shimon disagrees. He states that they limed the stones, and then wrote the Torah on the

The Inscription on the Stones 125

lime, which was a suitable material for this purpose. The Torah was therefore written in a revealed and open form. The verse states, "But you shall utterly destroy them: the Hittite and the Amorite, the Canaanite...in order that they will not teach you to do according to all their abominations" (*Devarim* 20:17–18). These words were written once in the body of the Torah in the appropriate place, and again after the last verse, at the bottom, to emphasize to the nations outside the land that this command did not apply to them. Their repentance would be welcomed and accepted.

A commentator on the Talmud points out that Rabbi Yehudah and Rabbi Shimon hold two opposing views about the relationship between the Torah and the nations. Rabbi Yehudah is of the opinion that the Torah is concealed from the nations; therefore it is appropriate to cover its words with lime. Theirs is a situation of unrealized potential; a barrier prevents them from having access to the Torah. However, they are blessed with *binah yeseirah*, and this enables them to peel off the lime and read the words of God.

Rabbi Shimon thinks otherwise. The nations' connection to the Torah is direct and open; accordingly, it was written *on* the lime.

Even though the altar was built and dismantled on the same day, the non-Jewish scribes were miraculously able to copy down the whole Torah in the time available to them. Another view is that the scribes wrote out the Torah after the stones were taken to Gilgal, and by virtue of a miracle the writing remained intact.

126   *Keystones of the World*

Teaching the Torah to Gentiles

This display of the Torah was not intended to persuade the gentiles to convert to Judaism, but they were expected to absorb basic tenets, such as the unity of the Creator. A question remains, however. It is written, "He declares His word to Yaakov, His statutes and His ordinances to Israel. He has not done so for any nation — and as for His ordinances, they have not known them" (*Tehillim* 147:19–20). We are not allowed to teach Torah to gentiles, so why did the Jewish people do so on this occasion?

One answer is that although it's generally forbidden, at that time it was permitted for the purpose mentioned earlier: to prevent a false claim on the Day of Judgment. An alternative explanation makes a distinction between the written law and the oral law: one may transmit the former but not the latter.

The Chosen Nation

The command to write the Torah in seventy languages might have aroused doubts in the hearts of the Jewish people. They would wonder, "Are we truly the *am segulah*? Maybe in the future God will abandon us and choose a different nation, a nation that has decided to obey the words of the Torah."

But any such misgivings evaporated once they had fully absorbed the details of this commandment. Lime covered the writing (according to Rabbi Yehudah's opinion), and the gentiles had to go to the trouble of scraping it off before they could read the Torah. This was an indication that the Jewish people had nothing to fear.

The Inscription on the Stones

127

There were further assurances. Moshe instructed the nation to build an altar and offer up *shelamim*, peace offerings, to show that there is peace between God and His people; they were to eat bread and meat and "rejoice before God."

"You shall write," "you shall sacrifice," "you shall eat" — these are all written in the second person singular and hint at the reason God chose the Jewish people — because their souls are united. The Jewish nation is one, like God Who is One, and His Name is bound up with His people.

"Explain [Them] Well"

"And you shall write on the stones all the words of this Torah; explain [them] well [באר היטב]" (*Devarim* 27:8). With this phrase Moshe indicated that the Torah was to be written in seventy languages. A truly full and complete exposition is one that is understood by every nation. This is indicated by the *gematriah* (numerical value) of the word היטב, which can be calculated as follows: ה (5) + היי (15) + הייט (24) + היייב (26) = 70 — the total number of languages spoken at that time. The word *all* in the verse quoted above signifies that all five books of the Torah were written on the stones. But how was this possible? How could they fit seventy copies of the entire Torah on twelve stones?

God performed three miracles in connection with the writing. First, the twelve stones, in defiance of natural laws, were capable of containing an immense amount of material. Furthermore, Yehoshua, who actually wrote out the Torah on behalf of the people, accomplished this

128 *Keystones of the World*

very rapidly, on the day they crossed the Jordan. Third, God taught him the seventy languages, so he was well equipped for a task that would daunt the most proficient linguist.

Normally the word for lime, סיד, is spelled with a *samech*. But here the letter *sin* is used, hinting at the divine command "That's enough!" (an anagram of שיד). God limited the size of the stones, and despite their relatively small proportions, they were able to hold all the material in a perfectly legible form.

A different opinion points out that the word גדלות in the phrase "large stones" is written in the shorter form, without the letter *vav*. The stones were originally very large, but they shrank to enable the twelve men to lift them from the river. Later they returned to their former size to serve as a suitable medium for the translation of the Torah in seventy languages.

Understanding the Repetition

The first thing one notices when reading these verses in *Ki Savo* is that there is a considerable amount of repetition. A number of commentators deal with this point and arrive at very different conclusions.

One opinion explains that it is simply a case of general statement followed by detail. Moshe introduces the subject with two sentences: "And it shall be on the day you cross the Jordan...and you shall erect large stones and coat them with lime. And you shall write on them all the words of this Torah...." Then he becomes more specific and enumerates all the relevant details. In this light we can understand, for example, why the first command

The Inscription on the Stones

129

to write on the stones precedes the instruction to build an altar, despite the fact that the Torah had to be written on the stones of the altar.

But another commentator gives a more complex explanation. In his view there were two layers of writing on the stones. On the day the Jewish people were to cross the Jordan, they set up the stones temporarily on a base, a method traditionally used to prevent such stones from moving while the work is being done. They then proceeded to plaster them with lime, a specific type of lime called שיד (spelled with a *sin*). This is unsuitable for building work but is ideal for a task of this nature. סיד, on the other hand (which is spelled with a *samech*), is used for constructing buildings.

By the time the people were about to enter the Jordan, the stones were partly dry and ready for the first inscription. This was done as they were actually crossing the river — וכתבת...בעברך, "You shall write...when you cross" — which is easier to understand when one remembers that God formed the waters into a wall. The stones were erected on Mount Eival and (according to this commentator) remained there for generations.

Once they were completely dry and hard, they were plastered anew with lime, and it was at this point that Yehoshua built the altar, and the people offered up sacrifices. The altar was constructed from different stones (according to this opinion), stones untouched by iron. But the first set was hewn and planed to enable the lime to be spread evenly over the entire surface. This ensured consistency in the depth of the writing.

By the time the people had finished eating the sacri-

130   *Keystones of the World*

fices, the lime was again half dry, presenting an ideal surface for writing — neither too soft nor too hard. The Torah was again inscribed on the stones, and their task was at last complete.

The upper layer was meant to be read by the nations of the time, and the lower, concealed inscription was intended as a backup for the future. Later generations might doubt that the writing was genuine; they would suspect it had been tampered with or damaged. The Jewish people would then be in a position to reply, "Peel off the top layer — you'll be able to read exactly the same version on the lower inscription."

But the two sets of writing were not identical. The upper layer was beautifully written in a highly professional manner, and its quality was such that it was impossible to tell whether it had been done the previous day or years ago. But by examining the lettering in the lower layer, an expert would be able to determine when it had been written, and that was exactly what was needed for future generations.

A different opinion explains this mitzvah in the light of the mores and traditions of the era. The Jewish people were inevitably influenced to an extent by the customs of the other nations. On entering a city, the non-Jewish conquerors would set up monuments in a display of confidence and self-glorification, as if to say, "We are masters of this land." They would write down their names and an account of their battles, along the lines of "King Ramon went to war against King Chemosh in the year...defeated him, and achieved a resounding victory."

The Inscription on the Stones   *131*

So Moshe initially told the people that he was well aware of what they intended to do when they would enter the Land of Israel. The earlier verses are not instructions, but a summary of what was going to happen. They would erect a monument of their own accord — "You will set up *for yourself*" — lime the stones in order to facilitate the writing process, and then describe their history: how they emerged from Egypt, received the Torah, wandered for forty years in the desert, conquered Sichon and Og.... This will all take place as a matter of course, "because you are entering the land."

But the Jewish people are no ordinary nation. When they set up their monument, it must be done with the noblest of motives — the desire to fulfill God's command and to glorify His Name, not to aggrandize their own. Moshe went on to tell them how to carry out this commandment: "Lift the stones from the Jordan and erect them on Mount Eival in the form of a monument. Then build an altar from some of the stones you used for the monument, offer up sacrifices, and eat and rejoice *before God*, Who has miraculously brought you to this land. After you have dismantled the altar, write down on the stones not merely an account of your history, but all the words of the Torah, including every commandment. And bear in mind throughout that you are doing this only to serve God — for that purpose and no other."

The Place of This Mitzvah in the *Chumash*

The verses preceding this mitzvah exhort the people to observe the precepts of the Torah: "This day Hashem your God commands you to do these statutes and ordi-

132   *Keystones of the World*

nances..." (*Devarim* 26:16). The strength of the evil inclination is so great that without help from the Creator we would be unable to keep the Torah. Similarly, miracles surrounded the mitzvah with the stones, and it is this supernatural assistance that links these two topics.

By performing this commandment, the Jewish nation gained spiritual strength and were thus prepared for the role of being God's people. The last verse about the stones is therefore followed by the words "This day you have become a people to Hashem your God" (ibid. 27:9).

Then Moshe gave instructions about a different mitzvah, one closely connected with the writing on the stones: "These [tribes] shall stand on Mount Gerizim to bless the people...and these shall stand on Mount Eival for the curse" (ibid., 12–13). After fulfilling the mitzvah with the stones, the Jewish people performed this ceremony exactly as Moshe had commanded. By answering amen, they swore that they would keep the Torah, the very Torah that was in front of their eyes at that moment.

❀   ❀   ❀

Part Three — The Performance of the Mitzvah

In *Ki Savo* Moshe issued detailed instructions that were to be carried out at a later date. Chapter 8 of *sefer Yehoshua* describes how this mitzvah became a reality.

> Then Yehoshua built [literally, "will build"] an altar to Hashem, the God of Israel, on Mount Eival, as Moshe, the servant of God, had commanded the children of Israel, as it is written in the book of the

The Inscription on the Stones

133

Torah of Moshe — an altar of whole stones upon which no [man] has lifted up iron. And they sacrificed burnt offerings to God, and they offered peace offerings. He inscribed on the stones a repetition of the Torah of Moshe, which he wrote before the children of Israel.

And all of Israel...stood...half of them on the slope of Mount Gerizim and half of them on the slope of Mount Eival, as Moshe the servant of God had commanded.... Afterward he read all the words of the Torah, the blessing and the curse, according to all that is written in the book of the Torah.

(*Yehoshua* 8:30–34)

When Yaakov spent the night in Luz, he took twelve stones from the altar that Avraham had built for the *akeidah*, the binding of Yitzchak, and placed them around his head (see chapter 2). They merged miraculously into a single stone, as a sign that he will father twelve tribes. Yaakov also inferred that his descendants will be as hard as stone in their battles against the nations, and this quality of unyielding strength would enable them to inherit the Land of Israel. But with regard to the commandments of the Torah, they would be as soft and malleable as wax.

Furthermore, this incident hinted at the importance of unity among the Jewish people. Only if peace and love prevail will they be able to defeat the enemy and inherit the land; causeless hatred and strife will result in exile.

Over three hundred years later God commanded Yehoshua to take twelve stones, corresponding to the

134   *Keystones of the World*

twelve tribes. Yaakov had removed the stones from Avraham's altar, and Yehoshua now bound together his own stones by building an altar. Yehoshua's stones were exactly the same size and weight, an indication that each tribe has to be equally diligent in keeping the Torah for the nation to be worthy of the Land of Israel.

"Then Yehoshua Built an Altar"

When did Yehoshua build the altar? Although these verses appear directly after the account of the battle of Ai, a number of opinions maintain that Yehoshua built the altar as soon as the people entered the land, as it states in *Ki Savo,* "*And it shall be on the day* when you shall cross over the Jordan...you shall erect for yourself large stones...and you shall build an altar there" (*Devarim* 27:2–5).

This is an example of the principle "There is no chronological sequence in the Torah." The events described in Tanach aren't always written in the order in which they occurred.

In the course of that day the people crossed the Jordan (which is near Gilgal), traveled over sixty *mil* to Mount Eival, built the altar, wrote out the Torah, and walked the same distance back to Gilgal. There they rested and set up camp for the first time in the Land of Israel.

Many miracles happened on this particular day, besides the splitting of the Jordan. First, the fact that they accomplished so much in the space of one day was in itself a supernatural occurrence. It normally takes eighteen minutes to cover one *mil* (about one kilometer or three-

The Inscription on the Stones 135

quarters of a mile) by foot, so one would expect sixty *mil* to take eighteen hours. Also included in the itinerary were liming the stones, writing the Torah in seventy languages, and reciting the blessings and curses.

Second, no one harmed the Jewish people as they traveled to Mount Eival; God granted them special protection. Neither man nor beast was able to attack the incoming nation, and anybody who tried was immediately seized with terror.

Furthermore, the twelve men carrying the stones didn't stop to rest despite their heavy burden. They kept up with the pace of the rest of the people and arrived in good time.

There were also a number of miracles in connection with the writing on the stones that have already been mentioned.

Others say that this sequence of events *is* written in the correct chronological order. Only after conquering the city of Ai did Yehoshua build the altar and write down the Torah. But surely the verse in *Ki Savo* (*Devarim* 27:2) specifies that this mitzvah should be performed on the day the Jewish people arrive in the Land of Israel.

However, the verses (*Devarim* 27:2–5) can be interpreted differently. The Torah states, "And it shall be on the day when you shall cross over the Jordan...set up for yourself large stones." The obligation to act on the same day refers only to erecting the monument in Gilgal. "And you shall coat them with lime, and you shall write on them all the words of this Torah when you have crossed over...and you shall build an altar there" [on Mount Eival] — this second mitzvah was performed later, not on the day they crossed the Jordan. The stones were carried from Gilgal to Mount Eival and then used to build an altar and display the words of the Torah.

A third view is that Yehoshua built the altar and wrote out the Torah after the land had been fully conquered and divided, not following the battle of Ai.

"Then Yehoshua Will Build"

יבנה, "he will build," is in the future tense and is preceded by the word אז, then. This form appears in a number of verses, especially at the beginning of chapters expressing joy and exaltation of spirit. Two other examples are אז ישיר משה ובני ישראל את השירה הזאת לה׳, "Then Moshe and the children of Israel sang [literally, 'will sing'] this song to God" (*Shemos* 15:1), and אז ידבר יהושע לה׳ ביום תת ה׳ את האמרי לפני בני ישראל, "Then Yehoshua spoke [literally, 'will speak'] to God on the day when God delivered up the Amorites before the children of Israel" (*Yehoshua* 10:12).

The Midrash tells us that the phrase "Then Yehoshua will build" is an allusion to *techiyas hameisim*, the resurrection of the dead. The future tense hints that Yehoshua "will build" again, when the time comes for the revival of the dead. Similarly, Moshe will once more sing praises to God in that future era. *Techiyas hameisim* is not mentioned in Tanach, because when something is very delicate and needs a fine spiritual appreciation, it cannot be expressed in the physical form of letters. This also applies to the World to Come, and both are referred to only in the oral law.

Although there is no mention of liming in these

The Inscription on the Stones 137

verses, one should not imagine that this part of the mitzvah was neglected. Yehoshua followed Moshe's instructions to the letter and did not omit a single detail.

"The Torah of Moshe"

> He [Yehoshua] inscribed on the stones a repetition of the Torah of Moshe, which he wrote before the children of Israel.
>
> *(Yehoshua 8:32)*

We know that the Torah was written on the stones in seventy languages, but what is meant by "Torah" in this context? The commentators give many answers to this question; here are five opinions:

1. The whole of the *Chumash* (Pentateuch) was inscribed on the stones, from "In the beginning" until "all of Israel." (Moreover, every letter was written with its crownlet.)

   The proof lies in the words of the verse "He [Yehoshua] inscribed on the stones a repetition of the Torah of Moshe which he [Moshe] wrote before the children of Israel." Moshe completed a *sefer Torah* for every tribe by his own hand, and Yehoshua, too, copied out the entire Torah onto the stones.

2. The phrase "a repetition of the Torah of Moshe" means the book of *Devarim*. *Devarim* is called "*Mishneh Torah*" because it repeats what has been said in the four earlier books.

3. The stones contained only the Ten Commandments. This is evident from the words משנה תורת משה אשר כתב לפני בני ישראל, "A repetition of the Torah of Moshe which he wrote before the children of Israel," a

reference to the Ten Commandments on the **second** tablets, which were inscribed by Moshe in front of the nation.

4. Yehoshua wrote down the 613 commandments of the Torah and nothing more.
5. The blessings and the curses formed the sum total of the inscription. This is implied by verse 34: "Afterward he read all the words of the Torah, the blessing and the curse."

The Talmud lists three sets of stones: those Yehoshua placed in the Jordan, those lifted from the Jordan and erected in Gilgal, and those set up by Moshe in Moav.

Moshe also wrote out the Torah on stones, and the Talmud derives this from a comparison between two verses. In *Ki Savo* we read, "And you [the Jewish people] shall write on the stones all the words of this Torah; **explain** [them] well [באר היטב]" (*Devarim* 27:8). The same key word is used in the following verse: "Beyond the Jordan, in the land of Moav, Moshe began to explain [באר] this Torah, saying" (*Devarim* 1:5). The Talmud therefore infers that Moshe, too, inscribed stones with the words of the Torah.

These three sets of stones encapsulate the three principles of faith.

The stones Yehoshua put in the Jordan as a memorial to the miracle teach of God's existence and His unique ability to renew the world and do with it what He wills.

The stones taken from the Jordan were inscribed with the words of the Torah and bore witness to the blessings and curses pronounced at Mount Eival. They

The Inscription on the Stones — 139

embody the concept of reward and punishment — reward if those words are heeded, punishment if they are ignored.

Finally, the stones erected by Moshe in Moav also displayed the words of the Torah; they illustrate the principle of its divine origin. These stones, which were inscribed by *Moshe*, hint at the central concept written upon them — that he brought down the Torah from Heaven.

Chapter Eight
David Vanquishes Golias

David was still a young shepherd when he defeated Golias, but he had already been marked out for greatness. In accordance with God's instructions, Shmuel HaNavi had anointed David as the next king of Israel. Henceforth David was imbued with the spirit of God; he was given a new strength, which equipped him for this formidable task.

Simultaneously this self-same spirit left Shaul, and he was stricken with a deep sense of loss. The moment David was anointed Shaul was in essence no longer king. He lost his God-given strength and sank into a black depression. In an ironic turn of events, David became his personal musician; when he played the harp, Shaul found relief from his anguish. Shaul loved David, unaware that this youth was the true king of Israel.

In *sefer Shmuel* I (ch. 17), we read of how the Philistine army gathered to fight against the Jewish nation. But instead of mobilizing in their own country, they chose to assemble in Yehudah, their enemy's territory. They sensed that Shaul had lost his strength and reacted with this display of supreme assurance.

Golias Challenges the Jews

From the ranks of the Philistines, a giant of a man stepped out. This was Golias. Who was Golias? What do we know of his origins?

It is written, "These four were born to Harafah in Gat, and they fell into the hands of David and into the hands of his servants" (*Shmuel* II 21:22). Harafah is Orpah, Naomi's daughter-in-law, and one of her sons was named Golias. The Talmud relates that in the merit of the four tears Orpah shed before she parted from Naomi, she had four children who were giants. But why was this particular reward appropriate? The Talmudic Sages say that crying causes a loss of strength. Since Orpah gave away her strength in four tears, she was deemed to deserve four extremely strong sons.

In the book of *Rus*, the verse says, "Orpah kissed her mother-in-law [before leaving her], but Rus clung to her" (*Rus* 1:14). God said, "May the children of the one who kissed fall into the hands of the children of the one who clung." And many years later, Orpah's four sons were killed by King David and his servants.

Kissing seems to be a weaker form of clinging, but in fact it is its opposite. Orpah kissed Naomi and went; she tasted holiness and rejected it. Despite being aware of Naomi's greatness, Orpah left and returned to her people and her gods. Turning her back on Naomi caused her spiritual level to fall lower than it had ever been before.

The verses vividly describe Golias's appearance:

> And there went out a mighty man from the camps of the Philistines named Golias of Gat, whose

142   *Keystones of the World*

height was six cubits and a span [over ten feet]. And he had a copper helmet on his head, and he was wearing a coat of mail; and the weight of the coat was five thousand shekels of copper [about 60 kilograms or 130 pounds]. And he had greaves of copper on his legs and a javelin of copper between his shoulders. And the hilt of his spear was like a weaver's beam, and the body of his spear weighed six hundred shekels of iron [between seven and eight kilograms or sixteen pounds]; and his shield bearer went before him.

(Shmuel I 17:4–7)

Golias was apparently well protected from any weapon or missile; his head, body, and legs were all shielded with armor. Besides being unusually tall, he was exceptionally strong, capable of bearing immensely heavy armor and weaponry. All this gave him the appearance of an invincible, intrepid warrior, and it was no wonder that he evoked fear in the hearts of his enemies.

The word for "hilt" is read as עץ, but it is written as חץ. The Midrash explains that the above verses describe barely half of his capabilities; the praise is only חצי, half. This teaches us that it is forbidden to praise someone who is evil. In this case, Golias's phenomenal strength is detailed in part for the purpose of pointing out David's bravery. One shouldn't praise a wicked person unless there is a positive purpose for doing so.

Golias stood between the Philistine camp and the Jewish camp and issued his challenge to the enemy.

David Vanquishes Golias 143

"Why are you preparing for war against us?" Golias called out. "War means that lives will be lost on both sides, many lives. So let's settle the matter through one-to-one combat. Let two fighters decide the outcome of this battle.

"Remember, I am the man who killed Chofni and Pinchas, and captured your Ark, the man who led our army into battle against you. Whenever you fought against us, you were defeated. You don't have a hope of victory. So listen carefully to my proposition.

"I myself will fight against anyone from your people, despite the fact that a prince doesn't normally stoop to fight a lowly commoner. Choose a man, a mighty soldier, and let him be my opponent.

"If he defeats me, then we will be your slaves. And if not — if I am the victor — then you will serve us. But why should that matter to you anyway? You are already slaves to Shaul, so if I win, you will merely change masters!"

No one responded to Golias's challenge. The people stood in silence.

So he continued, "Jews! I have insulted your army with my request. It seems there is no man among you who is capable of fighting me. Not one person has answered my challenge.

"If you want to wipe out this disgrace, let a man come forward, and we will do battle!"

Golias showed the contempt he bore for the Jewish nation in a number of ways. Addressing the people rather than their monarch was in itself an insult, since it is the king who fights the nation's battles. He demeaned the king and by implication his subjects. And he deliber-

144   *Keystones of the World*

ately called the Jews "slaves to Shaul," partly in order to disparage them, but also to incite rebellion against the king. He even reviled the God of Israel, but his words are not recorded out of regard for God's honor. In addition, anyone who insults the Jewish army insults God, because He walks in the camp of Israel (see *Devarim* 23:15).

Golias's formidable appearance and arrogant words inspired great fear in Shaul and the people. Shaul's strength had left him, and he was afraid. When the Jews saw that their king was frightened, they too were filled with dread.

It took both nations forty days to assemble their troops, and Golias lost no opportunity to hammer home his message. He stood in front of the camp of Israel and repeated the same words morning and evening.

The number forty is significant. The Jewish people waited forty days for Moshe to descend from Mount Sinai; this merit would enable them to defeat the Philistines. And Golias was permitted to live forty days longer because his mother Orpah walked forty steps together with Naomi.

David Resolves to Act

The verse introduces David as "the son of this man of Efras, from Beis Lechem, Yehudah, whose name was Yishai" (*Shmuel* I 17:12). These words hint at David's ancestry — the righteous Rus was his great-grandmother. How does the verse allude to Rus? In the book of *Rus* we read, "[The people said to Bo'az] 'May God make the woman [Rus] who is coming into your house like Rachel

David Vanquishes Golias   **145**

and Leah, both of whom built up the house of Israel. May you prosper in Efras and be famous in Beis Lechem' " (*Rus* 4:11). David came from Beis Lechem, as the verse notes specifically, and became very famous, in fulfillment of the blessing in *Rus*.

The Talmud says, ‏גלית...שעמד **בגלוי** פנים לפני הקב״ה...‏, Golias stood with chutzpah before God. He demanded, 'Choose for yourselves a man [*ish*] and let him come down to me!' " (*Shmuel* I 17:8). The word *ish* indicates God, as it says, "Hashem is a Man of war" (*Shemos* 15:3). In response, God declared, "I will bring about his downfall through *ben ish*, the son of a man!" This refers to David, who is described as a *ben ish* in the verse quoted above.

Was Golias literally challenging God?

A commentator on the Talmud explains that the word *ish* denotes absolute independence, the power to stand alone without the need for help of any kind. Hence this word is used in connection with God. Golias said, "Choose for yourselves a man," because he wanted an opponent who was totally self-sufficient — a person who possessed great strength. In his arrogance, he was certain that even someone of this caliber would not be able to defeat him — but he was wrong.

David was king of Israel, but since he was supremely fit for this position, he was unique even among kings. He was a *ben ish*, a king in the truest sense of the word. Everyone was dependent on him, and he stood alone, needing no one but God. This was the man to kill Golias and save the Jewish people from the Philistines.

Even though David had been anointed king, he didn't become haughty, nor did he act in a lordly way toward his brothers. "David was the *katan* (the youngest)" (*Shmuel* I 17:14) — he remained humble and treated them with all the respect due to older brothers.

As the youngest of eight boys, David had not joined his people in their battle against the Philistines. Yishai's three oldest sons had gone out to war, and no one else was needed to represent his family.

With David away from the battle front, how would God arrange the crucial confrontation?

> Yishai said to David, his son, "Take now for your brothers an *eifah* of this roasted wheat and these ten loaves...ואת ערובתם תקח"
>
> (*Shmuel* I 17:17–18)

The phrase ואת ערובתם תקח is interpreted in a number of different ways. In its simplest sense, it means that David was instructed to find out about the welfare of his brothers.

But the Midrash explains that it refers to a pledge, a pledge that stretches back to the time when Yosef was viceroy of Egypt. There was a famine in Canaan, and Yaakov told his sons to go back to Egypt and buy some food. However, they could not return without Binyamin. Having lost Yosef, Yaakov could hardly bear to part from his youngest son, but without food they would die. So Yehudah promised, ...אנכי אערבנו, "I will be a guarantor for him.... If I do not bring him to you and set him before you, then I shall have sinned against you forever" (*Bereishis* 43:9). Yaakov gave his consent, and Binyamin

David Vanquishes Golias

and his brothers went to Egypt.

When the goblet was found in Binyamin's sack, Yehudah begged Yosef to release his youngest brother. "For your servant became a guarantor for the lad.... And now please let your servant stay instead of the lad as a servant to my master and let the lad go up with his brothers" (ibid. 44:32–33).

Yehudah's pledge was fully redeemed in the days of Golias. Yishai said to his son, "The time has come for you to fulfill the pledge of your ancestor Yehudah. Go and release him from his pledge!" — ואת ערובתם תקח. David went out and killed Golias, thereby saving Shaul, a descendant of Binyamin.

In response to this courageous act, God said, "Your grandfather Yehudah pledged his life for Binyamin. You did likewise for Shaul, who is from the the tribe of Binyamin. I swear that I will set the Temple within [both] your border and the border of Binyamin."

Eager to carry out his father's instructions, David rose early in the morning, following the practice of the Patriarchs and the pious. He arranged for someone to take care of his sheep and then traveled to the battlefield and found his brothers.

While he was talking to them, Golias appeared, on schedule, to deliver his piece. For the first time David listened to this evil man revile God and his people: "And David heard" (*Shmuel* I 17:23) — and he decided to act. Earlier we are told that Yishai's three oldest sons went out to fight the Philistines, but to their discredit they were not galvanized into action, not on the first day nor on the fortieth. But David's heart was stirred immediately,

148   *Keystones of the World*

and he resolved to remove the *chillul Hashem*.

Then he overheard the conversation of the soldiers. They were talking of an announcement that had been made in the name of the king. It seemed that Shaul had promised great riches to anyone who succeeded in killing the Philistine as well as his daughter's hand in marriage. Moreover, the man who slayed Golias would free himself and his family from paying taxes and performing any kind of national service.

David turned to the men next to him and asked, "What will be done for the man who smites this Philistine?" (ibid., 26). He knew perfectly well, but he inquired in order to give himself the opportunity to say that he was prepared to fight Golias.

Then he continued with fiery words, "Who is this despised Philistine who has the audacity to revile God's army — who dares to imply there is no mighty warrior in Israel?" The Jewish people are God's army because they fight in His Name and with His help; our battles are His battles. And since they are God's army, the insult also extends to Him.

David was determined to wipe out the *chillul Hashem*, and now there was an additional incentive. Marrying Shaul's daughter would be a steppingstone to assuming his rightful position as king.

One commentator explains the exchange between David and the soldiers in a manner that illustrates how zealous he was in his desire to defend the Name of God. When David heard of the reward on offer, he was astonished. Surely a successful act of vengeance for the insult directed at God and Israel was in itself the greatest reward

David Vanquishes Golias

— of far more value than any possession or gift. So he exclaimed, "What will be done for the man who smites this Philistine?" Will he actually receive another reward for removing this disgrace from Israel? "He reviled the armies of the Living God" (ibid.) — surely any man who cares about the honor of God and His people will take action for their sake, not because of the promise of riches and other privileges.

The soldiers entirely agreed with David. But they pointed out that it was not a question of reward. "So it shall be done for the man *who smites him*," they replied (ibid., 27). The fact that he is capable of overcoming an opponent as phenomenally powerful as Golias shows he is an exceptional person, a man of great strength and valor. Someone of this caliber is certainly a worthy recipient of honor and riches and a fitting husband for the king's daughter.

Fraternal Objections

Eliav heard David talking to the soldiers, and when he realized what his brother intended to do, he grew angry. Since Eliav was the oldest, he felt responsible for David's behavior; it is the firstborn who guides his younger siblings and prevents them from doing wrong. And he considered David's plan to be the height of irresponsibility. He could not imagine how David could survive an onslaught from Golias, and he spoke to his brother sharply: "Why have you come down? And with whom have you left those few sheep in the wilderness? I know your wild behavior and the wickedness of your heart, for

150   *Keystones of the World*

you have come down in order to see the battle!" (*Shmuel* I 17:28).

David hadn't yet told him that he had been sent by their father, and Eliav suspected that he had come of his own accord. He also was inclined to think that David had carelessly left his sheep unattended, prey to wild animals and robbers. But we already know that David had done neither of these things. The verse specifically says, "He left the sheep with a keeper, and he lifted [the provisions] and went as Yishai had commanded him" (ibid., 20).

Perhaps it was with regard to Eliav that David wrote, "I became a stranger to my brothers and an alien to my mother's children" (*Tehillim* 69:9).

David answered, מה עשיתי עתה הלוא הלוא דבר הוא, "What have I done now? Surely it is a word" (*Shmuel* I 17:29). He protested that he had done nothing wrong. True, he had spoken to the soldiers as if he intended to fight Golias, but his talk was just a "word." Saying is not doing. David was anxious to silence Eliav, so he pretended that there had been a misunderstanding.

According to another commentator, Eliav's rebuke was an eye-opener for David. Eliav was taking this seriously — he obviously expected David to carry out his plan. Here was a clear hint from Heaven that it was no empty, grandiose idea, but a *davar* — something of substance. (*Davar* can mean both "thing" or "word.")

A different commentator suggests that David was implying, "I haven't done anything *now*, but later I will — because an important matter is at stake. Golias has insulted the army of God."

King Shaul's Response

Word reached King Shaul that David proposed to do battle with Golias, and a messenger was dispatched to bring the young shepherd into the presence of the king.

David said to Shaul, "Your servant will go and fight against this Philistine" (*Shmuel* I 17:32). The expression "your servant" is used three times in these verses, indicating the loyalty he bore toward Shaul.

But despite David's undoubted courage and confidence, Shaul did not want to let him go. "You have neither the strength nor the stamina to overcome Golias," Shaul told him. "You are only a lad. You are ignorant of the tactics and strategies of war, whereas your opponent is an experienced warrior."

But David *was* accustomed to fighting powerful animals. He then related a hair-raising episode, using the past continuous tense to convey that such events were a regular occurrence. (His feats were probably famous in Beis Lechem, and that was why he had been described to Shaul as "a mighty man of valor" — see *Shmuel* I 16:18). "Your servant was tending his father's sheep, and a lion came with a bear, and it [the lion or the bear] carried off a lamb from the flock" (ibid. 17:34). David had made a belt from the skin of the lamb as a memento of the incident, and he now pointed to his belt and said to Shaul, "This is it."

The beast had the lamb in its jaws, so he struck the predator and snatched the tender creature from its mouth. But the savage animal was not about to turn tail and flee. It reared up against David, intending to tear its

152   *Keystones of the World*

enemy to pieces. David seized its beard and lower jaw and killed it without the use of a sword.

But that was not all. גם את הארי גם הדוב הכה עבדך, "Your servant smote both the lion and the bear." גם, את and גם denote a threefold "inclusion." Besides slaying the lion and the bear, he also killed their offspring: two lion cubs and one bear cub.

At the end of his narrative David declared, "And this uncircumcised Philistine will be like one of them, because he has reviled the armies of the Living God!" (ibid., 36). He was determined to kill Golias just as he had killed the animals who preyed on his sheep, and the comparison he drew between man and beast expressed the contempt he felt for the Philistine.

One commentator offers the following insight. One could argue that man, by virtue of his intelligence and innate humanity, is a far more dangerous opponent than a wild animal. But David pointed out that by insulting the army of God, Golias had descended from the level of a man to that of a beast. He was left with nothing but brute physical strength. That being so, he, David, would be the conqueror. His Godly soul had dominion over the animal world, and it was this power that enabled him to slay the lions and the bears. Likewise, he would overcome the predatory Philistine.

Then he spoke further.

David Vanquishes Golias   *153*

David said, "God, Who has saved me from the hand of the lion and from the hand of the bear, He will save me from the hand of this Philistine." Shaul said to David, "Go, and God will be with you."

(Ibid., 37)

Why does the verse say, "David said"? It is quite clear from the context that he was still talking to Shaul, so why is this phrase necessary?

The Midrash explains that Shaul had interrupted David. This verse constitutes David's response. After David had described how he had made short work of a number of dangerous beasts, Shaul had asked, "And what makes you think you are capable of killing Golias?" He was not impressed by David's strength, because Golias was a man, not an animal, and man is governed by *mazal*, destiny. The Philistines had the upper hand over the Jews at this time, so Golias's *mazal* was in the ascendancy. Furthermore, unlike David's feral opponents, Golias was armed with extremely powerful weapons.

David replied that he had not intended to prove his physical strength. The incident was simply a sign — a sign that God would help him in the future. Shaul was convinced by this argument and gave David his blessing: "Go, and God will be with you."

The Midrash says that David was one of four righteous men who were given a *remez*, a hint or sign. Two paid attention to the sign, and two took no notice. Moshe and Yaakov ignored it, but David and Mordechai did not.

God told Moshe, "And put into the ears of Yehoshua" (*Shemos* 17:14) — give these instructions to

154   *Keystones of the World*

Yehoshua, who will divide the land. Yet at the end of his life, Moshe begged God to let him enter the Land of Israel.

Yaakov was assured by God, "I am with you, and I will guard you wherever you go" (*Bereishis* 28:15). Nevertheless, later he was afraid: "And Yaakov was very fearful" (ibid. 32:8). He thought he might have lost God's protection through sin.

Mordechai said, "Is it possible that a righteous woman like Esther should be forced to marry this evil man? Maybe this is a sign for the future. Esther will have the ear of the king, and the Jewish people might be saved through her."

David wondered, "Why should I be singled out to kill these wild animals? Perhaps the Jewish people will need someone to fight against a powerful enemy, and I will be the instrument that brings about their salvation."

So should a sign be ignored or heeded? One should pay attention to it if doing so will add to one's *avodas Hashem* (service of God). That was the case with David and Mordechai. Yaakov and Moshe, however, disregarded their signs and engaged in intense prayer. Had Yaakov felt that God would guard him, he wouldn't have pleaded to be saved from Esav. Likewise, Moshe would not have prayed to enter the Land of Israel.

Shaul's decision to let David go was also based on the following calculation.

If David killed Golias, well and good. But if Golias killed David, the people would still be able to do battle with the Philistines. There was no need to abide by Golias's words, "And if I defeat him...you will be slaves to

David Vanquishes Golias

155

us" (*Shmuel* I 17:8), because one of the warriors in question was only a slip of a boy. Who could take the outcome of such a ridiculous encounter seriously?

A different opinion examines the precise wording of Shaul's response. David said to Shaul, "God, Who has saved me from the hand of the lion...He will save me from the hand of this Philistine" (ibid., 37). David used the Tetragrammaton, the four-lettered appellation for God's Name, which symbolizes the attribute of mercy rather than strict justice. But Shaul replied, "*And God* will be with you." The conjunctive *vav* (an inclusive *and*) alludes to God's *beis din*, court of justice. Shaul was confident that even the attribute of strict justice would accompany David.

Out of concern for David's welfare, Shaul clothed him with his own garments, those traditionally worn by the king at the time of battle. He also gave David his armor and his sword, which naturally were of the finest quality.

David was perfectly willing to confront Golias dressed like this, but it wasn't in his power to do so. Since he was unused to wearing such heavy attire, he was forced to remove it.

However, the Midrash interprets this episode differently. Why did Shaul clothe David with his own garments? He could not fail to realize the disparity between their heights. He was tall ("From his shoulder and upward he was higher than any of the people"), whereas David was short.

Shaul's action was a gesture. When a king wishes to honor a man, he dresses him in his own clothes, and Shaul wanted to express the love and respect he felt for

David. But he assumed that practical considerations would oblige David to remove the garments, which could not possibly fit him.

Yet they did. There is an indication of this in the relevant verse, which says, "Shaul clothed David with his garments [מדיו]" (ibid., 38). This hints at the word כמדתו, "according to his size." A short man who was appointed king became tall. When David was anointed, he grew taller, but his increased stature made no real impression on Shaul — until David donned the royal garments. Then Shaul noticed. He noticed it acutely.

David saw that the clothes fit him perfectly, and he was filled with joy, for this was a sign of *malchus*, kingship. ויאל ללכת כי לא נסה — he wanted to fight Golias clad in these garments; he felt that until now he had not experienced *malchus*.

But when Shaul realized what had happened, he went pale. He understood the significance of this only too well, and he became jealous. David, perceiving Shaul's reaction, said, " 'I can't go in these because I am not used [to them].' And David took them off" (*Shmuel* I 17:39).

"I Come to You in the Name of God"

> He took his stick in his hand, and he chose for himself five smooth stones from the brook, and he put them in his shepherd's pouch, [namely] in the bag, and his slingshot was in his hand, and he approached the Philistine.
>
> (*Shmuel* I 17:40)

Between the two warring camps lay a valley. From

David Vanquishes Golias

the brook in this valley David took five stones. The water had worn down the stones until they were smooth. This was the ammunition David needed for his slingshot.

The stick was a ploy. Golias would assume David intended to strike him with the stick and wouldn't try to protect himself from the slingshot.

According to a different opinion, David's choice of weaponry shows his deep trust in God. He took with him only a stick and some stones, items that would be used to drive away a wild beast. Golias was no more than an animal in his eyes.

Why did David take *five* stones? The Midrash explains that one was for the sake of God. God said, "Did he not blaspheme before Me? I must have him killed." One was for the sake of Aharon. Aharon said, "I should avenge the deaths of the *kohanim*, Chofni and Pinchas whom Golias murdered." Three were for the sake of the Patriarchs. They said, "It's our duty to kill him because he reviles God's army and tries to destroy our children."

Armed with stick and stones, David approached the Philistine. The lad and the giant drew nearer and nearer to each other. Golias looked at David and was filled with contempt. Israel's finest fighter was nothing but an inexperienced boy! Golias noted his beauty and was doubly convinced that David could not possibly be a warrior worthy of the name. A true soldier was weather-beaten, and the inevitable exertion and fatigue had a harsh effect on a man's appearance. How could a pampered, tender lad be a match for the mighty Golias?

"The Philistine said to David, 'Am I a dog that you come to me with sticks?' " (*Shmuel* I 17:43) In fact David had only one stick, but in his anger and scorn, Golias seized on the plural. He could not see the stones, because they were still in David's bag.

Then he cursed David and the God of Israel. The Midrash lists ten sins that are punishable by *tzara'as*, a demeaning skin affliction, one of which is cursing God. Golias was therefore stricken with *tzara'as*, as David said, היום הזה יסגרך ה' בידי, "On this day God will deliver you into my hand" (ibid., 46). הסגרה is an expression used in connection with *tzara'as*, as in והסגירו הכהן — "The priest will lock him up" (*Vayikra* 13:5).

At the beginning of the encounter, Golias was approaching David, drawing nearer, so why did he suddenly demand, "Come to me"? The Midrash explains that the *tzara'as* prevented him from moving freely; it was as if the land had seized him. A later verse states, "And he went and approached David." He was able to walk, but only with difficulty; due to the *tzara'as* his progress was slow and deliberate. This was fortunate, because had Golias come too close, David wouldn't have been able to use the slingshot effectively, since it is necessary to aim from a distance.

But there is an alternative explanation for Golias's request. The Philistine was heavily burdened with a coat of mail and weaponry, and he was forced to approach David slowly. But when he saw that David was free from cumbersome armor, he called out, "Come to me, and I will give your flesh to the bird of the heavens and to the animal of the field!" (*Shmuel* I 17:44). David answered, "On this day God will deliver you into my hand," and Golias was so enraged by this reply that he could hardly

David Vanquishes Golias

159

wait to confront his enemy. He made his way toward David, but his pace was inevitably slow, frustratingly so for the angry Philistine.

We can now examine David's reply to Golias in more detail. First David exclaimed, "You come to me with a sword and with a spear and with a javelin; and I come to you in the name of the God of Hosts, the God of the armies of Israel, whom you have reviled!" (ibid., 45).

He expressed the same idea in *Tehillim* (20:8): "Some [trust] in chariots and some in horses, but we call out in the Name of Hashem our God!"

David was virtually unarmed because his weapon was the Name of God, which Golias had abused. With this Name, he would miraculously defeat Golias.

As mentioned earlier, when issuing his challenge, Golias had demanded insolently, "Choose for yourselves a man [*ish*]." By *ish* he meant God. David now responded, "I come to you in the Name of God" — I, as His representative, will fight you.

He continued to address Golias with the confidence and certainty borne of absolute trust in God: "On this day God will deliver you into my hand, and I will smite you and remove your head from upon you; and I will give the carcass of the camp of the Philistines on this day to the bird of the heavens and to the wild beast of the earth" (*Shmuel* I 17:46).

Golias had boasted that he would give David's remains to *"behemas hasadeh,"* the animal of the field, but a *beheimah* is a domestic creature and does not eat human flesh. When David heard this, he thought, *His mind is gone — he is mine!* In response David predicted, "I will

160   *Keystones of the World*

give the carcass of the camp of the Philistines...to the *wild beast* of the earth."

He emphasized that it was not his strength that would bring about this victory, but God Himself. Consequently, "all the earth will know that there is a God in Israel" (ibid., 46). The nations who did not believe in Divine Providence would now recognize that God protects the Jewish people.

Furthermore, "all this congregation will know that God saves not by sword and spear, because the battle is God's, and He will deliver you into our hand" (ibid., 47). The Jewish people were under the impression that God would save them through natural means, so they busied themselves with preparing weapons. But soon they would realize that it is God Who fights their battles. Man doesn't need to concern himself with weapons and war.

David's eloquent words made Golias extremely angry. Seething with impatience, he inched his way laboriously toward his opponent. David, under no such constraints, ran toward the Philistine.

"David stretched out his hand to the pouch and took from there a stone and slung it and struck the Philistine in his forehead; and the stone sank into his forehead, and he fell on his face to the ground" (ibid., 49).

Clearly God was with David — the first shot met its mark. But how could the stone enter Golias's forehead when he was wearing a protective copper helmet?

One answer is that the stone pierced the helmet and sank into his forehead. Alternatively, there was a small area that was not covered by the helmet, and the stone was destined, by the will of the Creator, to land precisely

David Vanquishes Golias

on that spot. According to a different explanation, when Golias bragged, "I will give your flesh to the birds of the heavens," he looked up in response to his own words. This caused the helmet to slip backward, and so David succeeded in hitting Golias's forehead.

Golias was struck on the front of his head, so why did he keel forward and land on his face rather than on his back?

The Midrash explains that since Golias fell forward David's approach to decapitate the giant was shortened by over twelve cubits. A Midrashic commentator notes that the manner in which Golias fell was a sign of God's affection for David. He did a little extra for him in order to show His love. Similarly, when Yosef was sold as a slave to some traveling merchants, God arranged for the camels to be laden with pleasant-smelling spices to enable him to enjoy their aroma.

The Midrash also states that an angel pushed Golias and caused him to fall on his face. The angel was performing the will of God, Who declared, "The mouth that reviled and blasphemed shall be stopped in the dust," as it says, "Hide them [the evil people] in the dust together; bind their faces in the hidden place" (*Iyov* 40:13).

Moreover, by falling forward, Golias unwittingly fulfilled the words of the verse "I will cast your corpses upon the corpses of your idols" (*Vayikra* 26:30). Golias worshiped a god called Dagan, and he wore its name over his heart. In his death he lay face down with the idol underneath him — a corpse above his god.

One commentator states that since Golias toppled forward, the impact of the blow could not have been di-

162   *Keystones of the World*

rectly responsible for his fall. If anything, the blow would have caused him to fall on his back. But he fainted from pain, his legs gave way, and he landed on his face.

The chapter continues, "So David prevailed over the Philistine with a slingshot and with a stone and struck the Philistine and killed him; and there was no sword in the hand of David" (*Shmuel* I 17:50).

This verse summarizes what happened. It tells us, "Understand the magnitude of this miracle!" With a mere stone and slingshot, David defeated a giant of a warrior who was armed with lethal weapons.

Another commentator explains that at a certain distance from Golias, David dispatched one stone ("with a slingshot"); when he was closer, he threw another by hand ("and with a stone").

A different view implies that this verse is not a recapitulation at all. It describes how David continued to attack Golias with slingshot and stones until he killed him. David then ran up to Golias, seized the dead man's sword, and cut off his head.

Alternatively, it was the sword that actually ended Golias's life. The blow from the stone would have eventually killed him, but decapitation shortened his final moments.

When the Philistines realized that their mighty warrior was dead, they fled in terror. Evidently they had no intention of fulfilling their part of the bargain, as stated by Golias, "If he is able to defeat me in battle, and he kills me, then we will be your slaves" (ibid., 9).

And now victory was at hand. The people pursued the enemy, and many Philistines were killed. The battle

David Vanquishes Golias

was won, and God's army had triumphed. David took Golias's head and brought it to Shaul. Then he carried it to the cities of Israel and spread the news to the people outside the war zone, including the women and children.

David put Golias's armor and weaponry in his house in Beis Lechem. But the sword was taken to the Tent of Meeting in Nov. There it served as a memorial to the great miracle God had performed for David and His people. Everyone who went to the Tent of Meeting remembered the miraculous event, and his trust in God was renewed and fortified.

Today we still have a reminder of how David vanquished Golias. The verse says, "Tzipporah took a sharp stone and cut off the foreskin of her son" (*Shemos* 4:25). Why do we now use a metal knife for circumcision rather than a flint, as was the ancient custom?

When the stone struck Golias, it pierced the metal helmet and sank into his forehead. Since metal is stronger than stone, this is contrary to the laws of nature. But the angel in charge of stone had made an arrangement with his colleague, the angel in charge of metal.

"On this occasion, let the metal be weaker than the stone," the angel pleaded. "Allow the stone to penetrate the helmet and sink into the head of the Philistine. And in return, I give you this assurance: from now on, only metal will be used for the mitzvah of circumcision."

So it was settled, and the result of their agreement is apparent until this day.

Chapter Nine
The Altar

The site of the Altar on the Temple Mount was hallowed from the beginning of time. Adam, Kayin, and Hevel all built altars in this place. On emerging from the ark, Noach did likewise — he offered up sacrifices in thanks to God for saving the world. The binding of Yitzchak was performed on the same spot, and about eight centuries later King David bought this piece of land from Aravna Hayevusi, as the site for the Altar of the Temple.

The Altar and its ramp were prefigured in Yaakov's dream (*Bereishis* 28:12–13). The ladder in the dream symbolizes the ramp, and the phrase "was set on the earth" refers to the Altar itself. "Its top reached heaven" signifies the sweet aroma of the sacrifices that rose to God. "Angels of God ascending and descending on it" is an allusion to the *kohanim*, who walked up and down the ramp. (The prophet Malachi even refers to *kohanim* as angels.) "And behold God was standing beside him" — *him* can also be translated as "it," namely, the Altar.

The injunction to build an altar appears in *parashas Yisro*, following the Ten Commandments:

> And when you make for Me an altar of stones, you shall not build [it] of hewn stone, lest you lift up

The Altar

165

your sword above it; then you have profaned it. And you shall not ascend by steps to My Altar, so that your nakedness should not be uncovered on it.

(Shemos 20:22–23)

The Midrash and other commentators expound the meaning of each phrase in a customary blend of halachah and ethics:

"And when [אם] you make...an altar of stones." The word אם is normally translated as "if," but here it means "when." It is obligatory rather than merely permissible to build a stone altar. We are equally obliged to lend money to a fellow Jew and to give our first fruits to God — and in both of these cases the word אם is used. Why are these particular commandments phrased in this manner?

When a person lends money, it should arise out of a wish to perform *chessed*, kindness, a wish he has deliberately implanted and nurtured within himself. Fulfillment of the commandment should emerge from his own goodwill. For this reason the Torah does not literally order us to observe this law. Likewise, the commandment of *bikurim*, the bringing of the first fruits, a tangible token of our gratitude to the Creator, is ideally a willing expression of appreciation that should not be felt as an obligation. Similarly, offering up sacrifices on the Altar should be done in the same eager spirit as *chessed* and *bikurim*. Although they are obligatory, the Torah wants us to carry out these mitzvos from personal choice, not because we have been so commanded.

"You make for Me." The Altar has to be built לי, "for

166   *Keystones of the World*

Me" — for the sake of the mitzvah. All the actions involved in constructing the altar, including transportation of the materials, must be permeated by the conscious intention of carrying out this commandment. The stones assigned for this holy purpose may not be used subsequently for something mundane. If they are defiled by idol worshipers, they become unfit for use.

In the times of the Chashmonaim, the Greeks offered up sacrifices to their gods on the Altar. In the process of cleansing the Temple, the Chashmonaim locked up the stones of that Altar in the northeastern chamber of the brazier room. There was no other option — the stones could not be destroyed, because they were once holy, nor could they be used, because they had been defiled.

The Altar is one of a group of thirteen expressly linked to God Himself through the use of the word לִי, "for Me." The others are silver and gold, the *kohanim*, the *levi'im*, the Jewish nation, the firstborn, the heave offering, the anointing oil, the Tent of Meeting, the kingdom of the House of David, the Temple sacrifices, the Land of Israel, and the Elders.

"You shall not build [it] of hewn stone." One may even use hewn stone to build the Holy of Holies, so it's natural to assume that this is permitted for the Altar, which is less holy. The Torah therefore explicitly states that it is forbidden.

A literal translation of this phrase reads, "You shall not build *them* of hewn stone." Since the Torah is referring to the Altar, why doesn't the verse state, "You shall not build *it* of hewn stone"?

The Altar

167

The word "them" alludes to the individual stones and it conveys an important halacha. Hewn stones as such are invalid, but do not invalidate the whole Altar; it is fit for use once the faulty stones have been replaced.

"Lest you lift up your sword above it; then you will have profaned it." The verse goes on to explain why hewn stone cannot be used for building the Altar. Tools for hewing are usually made of iron, and there is a powerful association between iron and physical violence. Weapons of war and destruction, typified by the sword, are made of this material. As one commentator expresses it, the hammer, which is made to smite the stone and hew it, is like the sword, which is made to smite man. The mason lifts up his tool, brings it down onto the stone, and hits it. He repeats this action until the stone splits.

The use of iron tools is therefore forbidden. This ban concerns the Altar rather than any other part of the Temple, and the Midrash explains why this is so. The Altar was created in order to lengthen man's life. By bringing sacrifices, he atones for his sins and merits God's blessing and long life. Iron, on the other hand, is used for exactly the opposite purpose, and it is not fitting for something that shortens life to have power over that which lengthens it.

The Altar can extend life, but we are nevertheless mortal because of the evil inclination. However, in the future, "He [God] will swallow up death forever..." (*Yeshayahu* 25:8).

Furthermore, through the sacrifices the Altar makes peace between the Jewish people and their Father in

168 — *Keystones of the World*

Heaven. Since the stones perform such an important service, they certainly "deserve" to be protected from iron, which cuts and destroys. These stones cannot see, hear, or speak, but since they bring peace the Torah commands, "You shall lift up no iron tool upon them" (*Devarim* 27:5). How much greater is the protection afforded to a thinking, feeling human being who makes peace between husband and wife and a man and his friend (or, on a larger scale, between nation and nation).

In a similar vein, the Talmud adds that surely no harm will befall those engaged in the study of Torah. The stones of the Altar atone for the sins of the Jewish people, but those who occupy themselves with Torah atone for the sins of the entire world.

"You shall not ascend by steps to My Altar, so that your nakedness shall not be uncovered on it." This verse teaches us the necessity of making a ramp for the Altar. Since it would be disrespectful to the Altar for the *kohanim* to take large strides, stairs are not appropriate. But there is another message underlying these words, one relating to our everyday behavior toward each other. Consideration is shown toward these inanimate stones — they serve a useful purpose, so they must not be treated irreverently. How much more so are we obliged to treat people with respect, every one of whom was created in the image of the Almighty. Since disrespect to man is tantamount to disrespect to God's image, one has to be extremely careful not to insult or shame anyone even to the slightest degree.

The Construction of the Altar

Before exploring in detail the reasons for these restrictions, let us describe the method of its construction. The Talmud tells us that the stones were taken from the valley in Beis Kerem, a village near Jerusalem. The stones in this valley were smooth and therefore suitable for the Altar. After digging in the untouched earth, they quarried whole stones that had never come into contact with iron. Since according to halachah the Altar was required to have a smooth surface, the stones were cemented together. If any part of the Altar was chipped, it became invalid (like a *shochet*'s knife), and the faulty section was replaced with a perfect one. Twice a year, before Pesach and Sukkos, the stones were whitened with lime. Iron trowels were not used for this task in case the iron touched the stones and rendered them unfit for use. Every Friday the Altar was cleaned with a cloth to wipe away any blood from the sacrifices.

The Talmud relates a dramatic incident that resulted in damage to the Altar. The Saduccees, a heretical sect who rejected the Oral Torah, were opposed to the Sukkos celebration of drawing water and pouring it on the Altar. This custom goes back to the times of the prophets, but since there is no allusion to it in the Torah, the Saduccees objected to it on principle. One Sukkos a Saduccee *kohen* poured water on his feet instead of on the Altar, in a deliberate display of contempt for the custom. The onlookers became enraged and pelted him with their *esrogim* (citrons). During the fracas, a corner of the Altar was chipped. The *kohanim* temporarily filled the gap with salt for appearance's sake, but the Altar couldn't be used until it was properly repaired.

The Reasons for the Restrictions

> When you make for Me an altar of stones, you shall not build [it] of hewn stone lest you lift up your sword above it; then you have profaned it.
>
> (*Shemos* 20:22)

When the commentators explain the rationale behind the verse quoted above, they present a twofold picture. First, what is the significance of whole, unhewed stones? Second, why is the use of iron forbidden?

The Significance of Whole Unhewed Stones

When a stone is cut, dust falls away that could easily be consigned to a trash heap. And the small chippings of stone left over might be used by the idol worshipers to build their altars. For part of a stone to be on the Altar and part in a refuse bin or a pagan temple was wholly unacceptable.

The very fact that idol worshipers used to cut stones for their altars is a further reason for the prohibition. In addition, if the masons were allowed to use hewn stones for the Altar, they would chisel them into the shape of the sun and the moon, and little by little the stones would come to represent a full-blown image for idol worship. But the Torah doesn't give this reason lest the ban be ignored. Disregarding human frailty, the masons would say, "We can build the Altar of hewn stone as long as we are careful not to make images."

The Altar   171

Another commentator makes an entirely different point. Earlier in *parashas Yisro*, when God gives the Ten Commandments to the Jewish people, He initially speaks to them directly, without using Moshe as a go-between. A little later is the injunction not to make gods of silver and gold — He must be served without any intermediary. He then instructs them to make an earthen altar, a simple altar involving very little labor, so they shouldn't imagine that their efforts brought about the blessings God bestows. Again there is the emphasis on the absence of a medium. Furthermore, the same applies to the stone Altar mentioned: it must not be made of hewn stone, the work of a craftsman, in order not to drive a wedge between God and His people.

A similar idea with a different slant is expressed by another commentator. The Altar was built purely לשם שמים, for God's sake. So it is only fitting that it should be made with stones in their original form, as they were created by God. Man's interference is not wanted here.

Finally, another reason for the importance of "whole stones" is directly connected to God Himself. God alone is truly complete. In order to indicate this, the stones that formed a focal point for serving Him were also complete.

God's goodness and wholeness aren't drawn from any outside source, and to act as a reminder of this He wanted the stones to remain as they are rather than being altered by the mason.

The Ban on Iron

In order to remind us that the Altar brings atone-

Keystones of the World

ment, blessing, and peace, we are commanded not to construct it with an element typically used for bloodshed and destruction. Man's thoughts are molded by his deeds, and building the Altar without iron tools will impress this message on his mind.

Bloodshed is personified by Esav, who hates God and is hated by Him. The word *cherev*, sword, is linked to *charav*, destroy. "By your sword you will live" (*Bereishis* 27:40) — this is the power and portion of Esav, and that is why iron shouldn't even touch the Altar. Even if a knife that has never killed anyone touches a stone, that stone becomes unfit for use. The slightest connection to strife is unsuitable for the Altar.

Moreover, an association between a symbol of punishment and a symbol of atonement isn't considered appropriate.

Why the Torah Prohibits Steps for the Altar

Since steps would cause the *kohanim* to take large strides, they may not form a part of the Altar. This command warns us not to behave in a lightheaded manner toward that which is holy and instills in our souls reverence and fear of God. The stones are not particular about how they are treated, but the prohibition impresses on our hearts God's great honor and importance. Building a ramp rather than steps drives this message home, because our thoughts are shaped by our actions.

God instructs us to build the Altar out of a basic inexpensive material — stone. But it is nevertheless essential not to treat it disrespectfully by making steps. In a general sense this also applies to the synagogue, which is de-

The Altar

scribed as a "small sanctuary." The building can be simple and modest, but one must not behave irreverently toward it by indulging in idle chatter.

לא תעלה במעלות, "You shall not ascend by steps," can also mean that we shouldn't try to "improve" the altar by placing on it gold, silver, and precious stones. These may seem to be מעלות, advantages, and thus eminently suitable in our eyes, but God tells us differently. We would thereby be leaning toward the customs of the idol worshipers, and there is no greater *ervah* (shame) than this.

The word במעלות, "by steps," hints at במעילות, "with sacrilege." Uziah, a king of Yehudah, was very powerful and successful, but unfortunately his great triumphs and strength went to his head. *Divrei HaYamim* relates that he entered the Sanctuary and burnt incense on the Incense Altar, an act that is forbidden to everyone except the *kohanim*. The *kohanim* ordered him to leave: צא מן המקדש, כי מעלת, "Go out of the Sanctuary, for you have committed sacrilege!" (*Divrei HaYamim* II 26:18). But instead of obeying, Uziah grew angry. *Tzara'as* broke out on his forehead. The *kohanim* quickly thrust him out, and he himself left with all possible haste because he realized God had punished him. He was forced to abdicate, and the affliction remained with him until the day he died. "You shall not commit sacrilege on My Altar so that your nakedness shall not be uncovered on it." In the case of King Uziah, it was *tzara'as* that exposed his sin for all to see.

The ordinary Jew was not even tempted to carry out such a brazen act, and a sin of this nature was hardly an everyday occurrence. He was more likely to be guilty of a

Keystones of the World

different kind of מעילות, by offering up a sacrifice in a spirit of falseness (for example, if he hadn't repented for the sin in question). God warns him, "Don't go to the Altar and ask the *kohen* to offer up your sacrifice, because I won't accept it. Your false-heartedness will be revealed to all the people standing below, because the smoke won't rise straight up like a pillar, as it normally does, and everyone will know your sacrifice has been rejected."

The stone ramp was thirty-two *amos* long (about sixty feet). Salt was sprinkled on it to prevent the *kohanim* from slipping. A combined hatch and shelf was installed on the western side of the ramp; this was used as a temporary storage area for the bird offerings that had become unfit for use (they were later burned).

Between the ramp and the Altar was a gap that led to a small recess. Wine would drip down and gradually accumulate in the recess, and at long intervals the children of the *kohanim* would crawl down the gap and scrape out the wine, which had evolved into a solid mass. This was then burned in a special ceremony.

The Importance of Humility

The final three verses of *Yisro* begin as follows: "You shall make for Me an earthen altar..."; "And when you make for Me an altar of stones..."; "And you shall not ascend by steps to My Altar..." (*Shemos* 20:21–23). These verses stress the trait that is a prerequisite to serving God — humility.

God commanded the Jewish people to build an earthen altar to emphasize the importance of simplicity

The Altar   *175*

and humble behavior. Furthermore, God did not want the Altar to have any association with the anithesis of humility, so He forbade the use of the "sword" — iron — in its construction. The sword denotes pride, as in the phrase "the sword of your arrogance" (*Devarim* 33:29). He likewise forbade steps, because there is an element of haughtiness in ascending in this manner; it is not the right atmosphere in which to offer up sacrifices.

The parashah ends with the words "so that your nakedness shall not be uncovered on it." This hints at the fact that arrogance always has within it an aspect of immorality, as the Sages of the Talmud say, "If someone becomes arrogant, he is considered to have transgressed all the laws governing forbidden relationships."

The *Sanhedrin* and the Altar

The topic of the Altar is immediately followed by the *sidrah* of *Mishpatim* (laws). What is the connection between the Altar and halachah?

The *Sanhedrin* used to sit near the Altar in judgment. This isn't actually stated anywhere in Tanach, but we see a pointer to this from an episode involving Yo'av. On being sentenced to death by the *Sanhedrin*, he seized hold of the Altar in an attempt to save himself. This indicates that he was in the vicinity of the Altar at the time.

An interesting reason is given as to why the *Sanhedrin* sat next to the Altar. The Altar symbolized a distancing from the three most serious sins.

First, murder. As explained earlier, a stone that has touched iron is unfit for the Altar because the latter has

Keystones of the World

been created to lengthen life, whereas iron maims and kills. We thus infer the extent to which we should separate ourselves from violence of any kind.

Second, idol worship. The heathens used to make images of hewn stone, so we are commanded to make an earthen altar or use unhewn stones.

Third, immorality. The Torah's wish for absolute modesty was indicated both by the garments of the *kohanim*, and by the requirement of a ramp rather than steps to the Altar.

The judges, "the eyes of the congregation," were responsible for dealing with capital offenses. Their proximity to the Altar would constantly remind them of the will of the Torah: man should dissociate himself as much as possible from these sins.

There is also a specific link between the ban on steps and *parashas mishpatim*. The juxtaposition of the two sends a message to the judges: "Be deliberate in judgment" (*Avos* 1:1). Don't take "large strides" in your thinking; proceed slowly and carefully before pronouncing the verdict.

The Altar of Today

"The Altar, three cubits high, and its length two cubits.... This is the table that is before God" (*Yechezkel* 41:22). The Altar is referred to as the *shulchan*, table, several times in Tanach. We are bereft of the Altar but not of its substitute — the table at which we eat three times daily. The Altar atoned through the sacrifices, which are an expression of gratitude to God. Today our sins are for-

The Altar

given when we eat with the aim of strengthening ourselves for serving God, and especially when we give thanks to Him for feeding and nourishing us.

Thus the symbolic connection between the Altar and the table is particularly strong during Birkas HaMazon (Grace after Meals), which is one reason why we cover the knives at this point. But on Shabbos we leave them as they are, in order to distance ourselves from the practices of the Saduccees, who believed that it's forbidden to use knives on this day.

One commentator explains in precise terms how to ensure that the table actually atones for our sins. Practice generous hospitality, be fully familiar with the laws about blessings in order to avoid mentioning God's Name in vain, set the table tastefully for Shabbos, *yom tov*, and Rosh Chodesh, eat the three Shabbos meals, wash before and after eating, don't speak unnecessarily between *mayim acharonim* and Birkas HaMazon, and concentrate on this prayer without swallowing the words. If anyone speaks coarsely or kills a fly at the table, he is considered to have done this in front of the Altar. We should conduct ourselves in a dignified and God-fearing manner and feel that we are sitting before God Himself.

Chapter Ten
The Temple

Because of his involvement with battle and bloodshed, King David was forced to forgo the honor of building the Temple. This extraordinary privilege therefore fell to his son, King Shlomo.

The ban on the use of iron tools applied only to the building of the Altar (see chapter 9), but King Shlomo went beyond the letter of the law, and in the entire area of the Temple Mount, "no tool of iron was heard" (*Melachim* I 6:7).

Selection and Preparation

It is written in the first book of *Melachim*:

> The king commanded, and they quarried large stones, rare stones, to lay the foundation of the house with hewn stone. And Shlomo's builders and Chiram's builders and the stonemasons hewed them and prepared the timber and the stones to build the house.
>
> (*Melachim* I 5:31–32)

Since it is common practice to use stones of inferior quality for the base of a foundation, King Shlomo specifically commanded the workers to choose אבנים גדולות אבנים יקרות,

The Temple

179

large and heavy stones, suitable in size and substance. This combination provided the strength needed for a solid foundation.

יקרות, heavy, can also be translated as "rare" or "precious." A quarry in a certain mountain provided stones of superior quality, and this was the source that was used for the Temple. Since the stones were unmatched by those in other quarries, they were deemed precious.

"Hewn stone" indicates that the surfaces were planed, and the corners formed into perfect right angles. The stones were then ready to be used for the walls of the Temple. The stones for the foundation were also prepared in the same way, although they were later covered over. What was the reason for this apparently unnecessary labor? King Shlomo was very particular about the House of God, even planing the stones that would remain unseen.

The גבלים, stonemasons, are so called because they precisely chisel the גבולות, borders, of the stone, which is the essential skill of masonry.

A later verse in *Melachim* reads:

> And the House, when it was built, was built of whole stone, transported, and neither hammer nor ax nor any tool of iron was heard in the House when it was built.
>
> (*Melachim* I 6:7)

The stones were quarried and hewn with the use of iron tools and then transported from the mountain to the site of the Temple. Since the hewing was kept to an absolute minimum, the stones were still large, but they were cut so accurately that they fit together perfectly.

Once on site the stones could no longer be altered, and were thus "complete," and ready to become part of the building. This is the meaning of the phrase "The House, when it was built, was built of whole stone." Some opinions say that they used the *shamir* instead of iron tools for the task of hewing the stones. The *shamir* was a worm-like creature that could burrow through stone.

Protruding from one of the walls of the Temple were several ledges on which the *kohanim* and *levi'im* would stand during guard duty. A bystander might easily assume that the ledges were chiseled out after the building had been constructed. But of course this was not the case, since the Temple was built of "whole stone." They deliberately used stones of different depths, with the result that there were natural steps in the wall.

The Midrashic Interpretation

The Midrash asks, why does the verse use the unusual word בהבנתו, "when it was built," rather than a simpler phrase, such as כשהיה נבנה?

The word בהבנתו hints at the miraculous nature of the whole process. The work was done by itself. The Temple was "built of whole stone, transported..." — the stones carried themselves, flew upward, and took their place on the row of masonry. The Midrash relates an incident about Daniel to illustrate that such supernatural events aren't really so surprising.

Daniel was thrown into the lions' pit, and a stone

The Temple

181

was placed over the opening to prevent him from escaping. The puzzle is that in the entire country of Babylon there were no large stones, as is apparent from a verse about the tower that was built there: " 'Let us make bricks...' And the brick served them as stone" (*Bereishis* 11:3). So where did they find this stone?

An angel descended at that moment and appeared in the form of a stone lion. It sat at the opening of the pit, as it says, "My God has sent His angel and has shut the lions' mouths, and they have not hurt me" (*Daniel* 6:23). The angel sealed the pit and also saved Daniel's life. If God performs a miracle like this for one tzaddik (righteous man), it is hardly surprising that His hand is evident in the building of the Temple.

It is written, "See a man who does his work with alacrity: he will stand before kings" (*Mishlei* 22:29). King Shlomo and the *Tanna* Rabbi Chanina ben Dosa shared the trait of *zerizus*, eagerness to perform the will of God. But like so many tzaddikim, Rabbi Chanina was poor. On one occasion everyone from his town was offering up sacrifices in Jerusalem, but he was not able to participate. He longed to perform this mitzvah, but his poverty prevented him from doing so. *Should I be the only one not to bring a sacrifice?* he asked himself.

He thought of a unique solution. In a field at the bottom of the town he found a stone. He cut, planed, and polished it and resolved to take it to Jerusalem as a subsitute for a sacrifice. Since it was too heavy for one person to carry, he decided to hire workers who would take it for him. He came across five men and asked them, "Will you carry this stone to Jerusalem?" They replied, "If

182   *Keystones of the World*

you give us fifty *sela'im*, we'll do it."

This was a great sum of money that was totally beyond his means. Before refusing, however, Rabbi Chanina looked in his pocket. Perhaps God had miraculously provided the money he needed. But it was not to be found, so the men went away.

God then sent five angels in human form. Rabbi Chanina asked them the same question. They said, "Give us five *sela'im*, and we'll take it to Jerusalem. But you must also give us your hand and finger."

The angels wanted to convey the impression that Rabbi Chanina was helping them, but their intention was to lift both him and the stone. He obediently stretched out his hand, and they found themselves standing in Jerusalem.

There was still the matter of the five *sela'im*, and Rabbi Chanina was anxious to pay what was due. But the angels were not to be found. Troubled, he went to the Temple to speak to the *Sanhedrin*. What should he do about the five *sela'im* he owed?

They answered, "It seems that ministering angels brought your stone to Jerusalem. If you would have known they were angels, you wouldn't have agreed to pay, since you know they do not want money. This being so, you may keep the five *sela'im*."

It was said of Rabbi Chanina, "See a man who does his work with alacrity: he will stand before kings...." The interpretation in this context is not מלכים, kings, but מלאכים, angels. Rabbi Chanina's zeal to perform this mitzvah was noted by God, and He sent angels to assist him. (The words of this verse can also be understood differently. If you see a man accomplishing his work unnaturally quickly, it is because angels are with him, helping him.)

King Shlomo's eagerness to build the House of God was rewarded by angels appearing to him on many occasions. Furthermore, he was granted the privilege of writing *Shir HaShirim, Mishlei,* and *Koheles.*

According to a different opinion, it appeared that the Temple built itself, but in fact this was the work of the angels and the spirits, who willingly helped with this holy task. The Temple was bound up with God's honor and glory, so they too were drawn to participate.

But another reason is given as to why the spirits were so anxious to help, and this also explains why they confined their efforts to the Temple and did not take part in the construction of the *Mishkan.* It is written, "And all the labor was finished" (*Melachim* I 7:51). With the completion of the Temple, the work of the six days of Creation was finally at an end. The spirits, beings without any physical form, were created just before the beginning of Shabbos, "at the last minute." Dissatisfied with their bodiless state, they regarded themselves as unfinished and eagerly built the Temple in the hope that the time was ripe for them to receive bodies.

The *Shamir*

The Talmud tells us about a small creature called the *shamir,* which was the size of a barleycorn. It resembled a worm and was created, like the spirits, at twilight on the sixth day of Creation.

184   Keystones of the World

The *shamir* had the power to cut the hardest of materials and was even capable of splitting a mountain. Some opinions say that the *shamir* cut the stones for the Temple, but everyone agrees it was used to engrave the stones of the *choshen* (the *kohen gadol*'s breastplate). After the destruction of the Temple (whether it was the first or the second isn't clear), the *shamir* was no longer available.

A steel cage would be no barrier to this creature, so how did they prevent it from escaping? The *shamir* couldn't penetrate soft materials, so it was wrapped in balls of spongy wool, and placed in a leaden tube filled with barley bran.

The *shamir* had the unique privilege of cutting the stones for the *choshen*. The letters had to be engraved rather than written ("the engravings of a signet" — *Shemos* 28:21), and nothing from the stone could be lost in the process ("in their fullness" — ibid., 20), which ruled out the use of a cutting tool.

The *shamir* was the ideal instrument for this task. The letters were drawn in ink on the surface of the stone, and the *shamir* was then placed on top of it. By following the lines of the ink, it engraved the stones, and not even the tiniest fragment fell away.

The *shamir* was well guarded, but how did King Shlomo find it in the first place? The verse says, "[Shlomo] spoke of the animal and of the bird" (*Melachim* I 5:13). According to one commentator, the bird refers to an eagle. Shlomo asked the eagle for the whereabouts of the *shamir*, and the eagle brought it to him from Gan Eden.

But the Talmud describes a lengthier and more diffi-

The Temple
185

cult quest in search of the elusive *shamir*. (The following narrative is a blend of the Talmudic account and a symbolic interpretation.) King Shlomo initially consulted the Sages and asked them, "Where is the *shamir*?" He was advised to summon two demons, a male and a female; these creatures of the spirit were familiar with such matters. (He preferred not to use the *urim v'tumim* if other methods were available.)

By utilizing the scepter of God's Kingship, Shlomo had gained mastery over both the lower and upper worlds. He was therefore capable of dealing with the spirits on his own terms and could use force if necessary. But even when he applied pressure to the demons, they insisted they did not know where it was. However, they did say that Ashmedai, the king of the demons, might be more knowledgeable on this point than they were. Ashmedai lived in a certain mountain, and the demons went on to describe his daily routine.

"Every day he ascends to Heaven to study in the Heavenly academy. Then he returns here to study in the earthly academy. When he has finished learning, he goes to the mountain and stops by the side of his pit, a sealed pit that he has dug and filled with water. The entrance is covered with a rock and his personal signet. He checks that the seal is intact and undiscovered by any man, lifts off the rock, and drinks. He then covers the pit, reseals it, and leaves."

A commentator explains that a demon is a composite of an earthly and a Heavenly being. Because of his dual nature, he has a foot in each camp, and studies and understands both regions. After studying both the upper and lower regions, he imbibes what he needs (expressed by the word *drinking*). Like man, he has certain requirements, but humans are supplied with their needs en masse, whereas each demon receives what is specifically meant for him. Consequently Ashmedai had his own individual seal (but again this isn't meant literally).

Since it wouldn't have been fitting or dignified for the king himself to try to capture Ashmedai, Shlomo sent Benayahu ben Yehoyada as an emissary. Benayahu would act as a conduit for the king's spiritual power. Shlomo armed him with a chain on which was inscribed God's Name, some bundles of wool, and a few bottles of wine.

Benayahu found Ashmedai's haunt and began his work. He dug a second pit in the slope below Ashmedai's, made a small opening between the two, and siphoned the waters from Ashmedai's pit into the new one. Then he plugged the opening with the bundles of wool. After digging another pit above Ashmedai's, he poured wine into it, allowing the liquor to descend into Ashmedai's pit through a small opening he fashioned between the two.

Shlomo's plan was to undermine Ashmedai's strength by exchanging the water for wine. Since demons epitomize the quality of simplicity, they need water, a basic life source — not water itself, but its spiritual aspect.

Ashmedai returned and examined the seal to see if it was intact. It was. But on uncovering the pit, he immediately noticed that it contained wine instead of water. Benayahu was watching him from a nearby tree to see what would happen, but it seemed that the king of the

The Temple

demons was not to be caught so easily. Ashmedai rejected the wine with vigor. But he grew terribly thirsty and could no longer restrain himself. He drank, became intoxicated, and then fell asleep. This further reduced his powers because "sleep is one-sixtieth of death."

Benayahu emerged from his hiding place and quickly threw the chain on Ashmedai, closing it around his neck. The demon awoke and started to struggle, but Benayahu called out, "Your Master's Name is upon you!" By using God's Name, which is identified with the Jewish nation, a Jew is able to dominate the spirits. Thus Ashmedai was caught with no means of escape.

Benayahu now had the task of dragging Ashmedai back to King Shlomo. Along the way, Ashmedai rubbed against a palm tree, which he uprooted and flicked aside. He accorded similar treatment to a house that crossed his path. A widow who was living nearby saw the destruction wreaked by Ashmedai and begged him to spare her small hut. Ashmedai didn't ignore her plea. He moved his shoulders to avoid the hut, but this caused one of his bones to break. He exclaimed, "A soft tongue breaks a [hard] bone!" (*Mishlei* 25:15).

Paradoxically it was Ashmedai's strength that was the agent of his injury. A demon's strength lies in his simplicity, and the widow possessed the quality of lowliness, a trait akin to his. Due to their fundamental affinity, she was able to harm Ashmedai.

Ashmedai then noticed a blind man who was losing his way, and he set him on the right path. He did the same for a drunkard. When they saw a wedding party rejoicing, he wept. They overheard a man telling his shoe-

188   *Keystones of the World*

maker, "Make me a pair of shoes that will last for seven years!" Ashmedai burst out laughing and reacted in the same manner when they saw a sorcerer practicing his craft.

Later Benayahu questioned Ashmedai about his behavior.

"Why did you guide the blind man?"

"There was an announcement in Heaven that he is totally righteous, and anyone who helps him will merit a share in the World to Come."

"And why did you guide the drunkard?"

"They said in Heaven that he's completely evil. I gave him a measure of comfort in this world, so he would use up his reward for any good deeds he has done."

"Why did you cry when you saw the wedding party?"

"I knew the husband was destined to die within thirty days. The bride will have to wait thirteen years for the *yavam*, the man's brother, to reach adulthood before she can marry him."

"Why did you laugh at that man's request?"

"That man may not have seven days to live, and he wants shoes that will last for seven years!"

"Why did you laugh at the sorcerer?"

"He was sitting on top of a king's secret treasure room. Let him use his magic to discover what's underneath him!"

Finally they reached Jerusalem, but it was almost three days before Ashmedai was summoned to appear before the king. At the end of the first day, he asked his gaolers, "Why hasn't the king sent for me?"

The Temple

189

They answered, "King Shlomo has had too much to drink." On the following day Ashmedai asked the same question. "He has overeaten," the gaolers told him.

The purpose of the delay and these surprising answers was to make Ashmedai aware of the distinction between a human being and a demon. Man differs from a demon with regard to his body and his mind. Drink confuses a man's mind, and too much food damages his body.

At the end of the third day Shlomo summoned Ashmedai. Taking hold of a reed, Ashmedai measured off a piece four cubits long and threw it in front of the king.

"When you die," Ashmedai said, "you won't have anything in this world except the four cubits of your burial plot. Meanwhile you have conquered the entire world. Weren't you satisfied until you conquered me as well?"

"I don't want anything from you for my sake," King Shlomo answered. "I'm not motivated by arrogance. But I do want to build the Temple for the sake of God's honor, and for that I need the *shamir*."

Ashmedai replied, "The *shamir* hasn't been entrusted to me — it was given to the ruler of the sea. And he could only have given it to the wild cock, whom he trusts to keep its oath and return the *shamir*, as it has sworn to do."

As elucidated by the commentator, the *shamir* was given to the ruler of the sea because of the attraction of opposites. When the Jews were taking leave of the Egyptians, the sea was parted and stood still; it was deprived of movement, its very essence. By contrast, the *shamir's*

190 *Keystones of the World*

strength lies in its power to cut and split.

Similarly, the ruler of the sea passed it on to the wild cock because the two are opposite forces. The sea has the capacity to wipe out human habitation by covering the land; during Creation God commanded the waters to gather in one place to enable the dry land to appear. The wild cock, on the other hand, actively promotes human life and sustenance through the agency of the *shamir*. It carries the *shamir* to a mountain lacking vegetation and places it on the peak. The *shamir* does its work, and the mountain cracks open. The cock then collects seeds from the trees, brings them to the mountaintop, and tosses them into the cleft. In time the mountain becomes filled with vegetation.

But why was the *shamir* entrusted to the wild cock? The relationship in this case is between like and like. The *shamir* can cut the hardest material, and the wild cock is a very powerful creature. Unusual strength is the characteristic that links the two.

Armed with the information imparted by Ashmedai, Shlomo's servants searched until they found the nest of a wild cock with young. While the cock was away, they covered its nest with clear glass and awaited developments. When the wild cock returned, it tried without success to enter the nest. As they had hoped, it flew away and returned with the *shamir*, with the intention of placing it on the glass. One of the servants shouted at the wild cock in order to frighten it. The cock dropped the *shamir*, and the servant took it. In its anguish at losing the *shamir*, the cock choked itself to death. It had violated its oath to return the *shamir* to the master of the sea.

The Temple   191

The commentator explains that the essence of nature is continuation without change, adherence to age-old patterns of behavior. The *shamir*'s natural home at this point was with the wild cock because of the affinity that existed between the two. Until now all the *shamir*'s activities had taken place within the framework appropriate for this creature, and in that sense it wasn't fitting for the *shamir* to be in man's domain, which was outside its natural habitat. Consequently, the wild cock was distressed that it had broken its oath and failed to maintain the status quo. But King Shlomo ruled over the demons and the supernatural world and was therefore ultimately able to capture the *shamir*.

> Ten things were created on the eve of the Sabbath, at twilight. They are the mouth of the earth [which swallowed up Korach], the mouth of the well, the mouth of [Bilam's] donkey, the rainbow, the manna, the staff, the *shamir*, the script [the form of the letters engraved on the tablets], the stylus [the instrument used by God to engrave the tablets], and the tablets. Some say also destructive spirits, Moshe's grave, and the ram of our father Avraham, and some also say tongs, which can only be made with tongs.
>
> (*Avos* 5:8)

These ten phenomena correspond to the ten utterances with which God created the world. The *shamir*, being a worm, is linked to the command "Let the waters teem with creeping living creatures" (*Bereishis* 1:20).

They are also connected to the ten *sefiros* (divine emanations). The *shamir* corresponds to *chessed* (kindness), which is the antithesis of war, violence, and iron weaponry. Because of its role as a subsitute for iron tools, the *shamir* is identified with this *sefirah*.

Why was this diverse group created at twilight on the eve of Shabbos?

First, God created everything that would be in constant or regular use, and only at twilight on the sixth day were these ten phenomena brought into existence. The latter would be needed only at certain times or for one generation. Since they were of minor importance compared to the rest, their creation was delayed until the last minute.

Furthermore, by twilight Adam had sinned, and the evil forces were waxing in strength. To enable His people to ascend once more, God in His kindness created these ten phenomena for the benefit of the Jewish people. The time itself is particularly suited to protect them, because of the merit they gain from adding part of the weekday onto the holy Shabbos. It was the destiny of the *shamir* to wait some thousands of years before playing its crucial role for the *Mishkan* and the *Beis HaMikdash*.

Glossary

Akeidah — the binding of Isaac

Am segulah — cherished people

Aron — the holy Ark

Aseres HaDibros — Ten Commandments

At-bash — an alphabetical system whereby the first Hebrew letter, *alef*, corresponds to the last letter, *tav*; the second letter, *beis*, to the penultimate letter, *shin*; and so on.

Avos — Patriarchs, or Ethics of the Fathers, a section of the *Mishnah*

Beis din — Jewish court of law

Beis HaMikdash — the Temple

Bemidbar — Numbers

Ben ish — the son of a man

Bereishis — Genesis

Birkas HaMazon — blessings said after eating bread

Chashmonaim — Hasmoneans

Chillul Hashem — profanation of God's Name

Choshen — the high priest's breastplate

194   *Keystones of the World*

Chumash — the Pentateuch

Devarim — Deuteronomy

Divrei Hayamim — Chronicles

Eichah — Lamentations

Eival — Ebal

Even shesiyah — the foundation stone on the Temple Mount

Gan Eden — the Garden of Eden

Halachah — Jewish law

Hashem — God

Hevel — Abel

Ish — a man

Iyov — Job

Kayin — Cain

Kesubah — marriage contract

Ki Savo — a *sidrah* in *Devarim*, chs. 26–29

Koheles — Ecclesiastes

Kohen (pl. *kohanim*) — priest(s)

Kohen gadol — high priest

Levi'im — Levites

Luchos — the stone tablets that were inscribed with the Ten Commandments

Mayim acharonim — Water used to wash one's hands before reciting *Birkas HaMazon*

Me'aras HaMachpeilah — the Tomb of the Patriarchs in Hebron

Glossary

Melachim — Kings

Mesorah — the precise wording, spelling, and punctuation of the biblical text according to ancient tradition

Mezuzah (pl. *mezuzos*) — a parchment scroll containing texts from *Devarim* which is affixed to the doorpost

Midrash — a body of exposition on Tanach composed by the Sages of the Talmud

Midrash Rabbah — a major Midrashic work

Mishkan — the holy Tabernacle

Mishlei — Proverbs

Mishnah — the first section of the oral law

Mitzvah (pl. *mitzvos*) — Torah commandment or good deed

Parashah — see *sidrah*

Pesach — the festival of Passover

Pirkei Avos — Ethics of the Fathers, a section of the *Mishnah*

Rivkah — Rebecca

Rosh Chodesh — celebration of the new moon

Sefer Torah — a parchment scroll of the Pentateuch

Shechinah — Divine Presence

Shemos — Exodus

Shir Hashirim — Song of Songs

Shlomo — Solomon

Shmuel Hanavi — the prophet Samuel

Shochet — ritual slaughterer

Sidrah — a fixed section of the Pentateuch

Sukkos — the festival of Tabernacles

Tanach — an acronym for *Torah* (Pentateuch), *Nevi'im* (Prophets), and *Kesuvim* (Writings), the three sections of the Bible

Tanna (pl. *Tannaim*) — Talmudic Sage(s)

Tehillim — Psalms

Tumim — *see urim v'tumim*

Tzaddik — righteous man

Urim v'tumim — the inscription of the divine Name that was placed in the *choshen* of the *kohen gadol* and served as an oracle

Vayikra — Leviticus

Yaakov Avinu — our forefather Jacob

Yavam — the surviving brother of a woman's deceased husband (see *Devarim*, ch. 25)

Yechezkel — Ezekiel

Yehoshua — Joshua

Yeshayahu — Isaiah

Yirmeyahu — Jeremiah

Yishai — Jesse

Yisre'eilim — Israelites, Jews who are not Priests or Levites

Yisro —Jethro

Yitzchak — Isaac

Yom Tov — Festival

Sources

Chapter 1: The Foundation Stone of the World

1. Mishnah:
   Yoma 5:2.

2. Commentaries on Mishnah:
   Tiferes Yisrael; Rav Pinchas Kehati.

3. Gemara (with *Rashi*):
   Berachos 62b; *Yoma* 53b, 54b.

4. Midrash and *Zohar*:
   Bereishis Rabbah 79:7; *Vayikra Rabbah* 20:4; *Shir Hashirim Rabbah* 3:18; *Midrash Tanchuma, Pekudei* 3, *Acharei Mos* 3, *Kedoshim* 10; *Pirkei D'Rabbi Eliezer,* chs. 10 and 35; *Midrash Shmuel* 31:4; *Midrash Tehillim* 17:4; *Zohar, Vayechi* 231a.

5. Commentaries on Midrash:
   Eitz Yosef; Maharzav; Yefei To'ar; Radal.

6. Commentaries on Tanach:
   Radak; Torah Sheleimah on *Bereishis* 28:22; *Malbim; Da'as Mikra.*

7. Explanations on Tanach:
   Rav Elozor Reich.

Chapter 2: Yaakov's Pillar

1. Midrash:

Bereishis Rabbah 68:13; *Midrash Tehillim* 91:6; *Midrash Tanchuma HaYashan* (Buber), *Vayeitzei* 4; *Midrash Lekach Tov, Vayeitzei* 11; *Pirkei D'Rabbi Eliezer* 35; *Yalkut Shimoni, Iyov* 5.

2. Commentaries on Midrash:

Matnos Kehunah; Maharzav; Yefei To'ar; Eitz Yosef; Radal.

3. Commentaries on Tanach:

Rashi; Torah Sheleimah.

Chapter 3: The Stone on the Mouth of the Well

1. Midrash:

Bereishis Rabbah 70:8; *Pirkei D'Rabbi Eliezer*, ch. 36.

2. Commentaries on Midrash:

Eitz Yosef; Yefei To'ar; Matnos Kehunah; Yedei Moshe; Maharzav; Radal.

3. Commentaries on Tanach:

Ramban; Ba'al HaTurim; Rabbeinu Bachai; Seforno; Abarbanel; Rashi; Alshich; Or HaChaim; Malbim; Kli Yakar; Torah Sheleimah.

4. Explanations on Tanach:

Rav Dov Sternbuch.

Sources 199

Chapter 4: The Stone of Israel

1. Gemara:
   Sotah 36b

2. Commentaries on Tanach:
   Targum Onkelos; Rashi; Ramban; Rashbam; Abarbanel; Torah Sheleimah; Haksav V'Hakabbalah; HaAmek Davar.

Chapter 5: The Tablets

1. Gemara:
   Nedarim 38a; *Eruvin* 54a.

2. Midrash:
   Shemos Rabbah 41:6–9; *Shemos Rabbah* 46:1–2, 4; *Midrash Tanchuma, Ki Sissa* 16, 29–30.

3. Commentaries on Midrash:
   Eitz Yosef; Yefei To'ar; Maharzav; Radal on *Pirkei D'Rabbi Eliezer* 45.

4. Commentaries on Tanach:
   Baal HaTurim; Rashbam; Abarbanel; Rabbeinu Bachai; Seforno; Rashi; Ramban; Yalkut Me'am Lo'ez; Peirush Yonasan; Alshich; Da'as Mikra; Haksav V'Hakabbalah; Or HaChaim; Malbim; Torah Sheleimah; Meshech Chochmah; Mei HaShilo'ach; Kli Yakar; Yalkut Lekach Tov al Parshiyos HaShavua.

5. Explanations on Tanach:
   Rav Dov Sternbuch.

Chapter 6: The Rock of Kadesh

1. Gemara:

Sanhedrin 110a.

2. Midrash:

Bereishis Rabbah 99:5; *Bemidbar Rabbah* 19:5–6; *Midrash Tanchuma, Chukas, 9, 10; Yalkut Shimoni, Chukas* 20 (764).

3. Commentaries on Midrash:

Maharzav; Eitz Yosef; Matnos Kehunah.

4. Commentaries on Tanach:

Rashi; Rabbeinu Bachai; Tosafos HaRosh; Seforno; Ksav Sofer; Torah Temimah; HaKsav V'Hakabbalah; Meshech Chochmah; Divrei Shaul; Da'as Mikra; Yalkut Me'am Lo'ez; Ma'or VaShemesh.

Chapter 7: The Inscription on the Stones

1. Gemara:

Tosefta, Sotah 8; *Sotah* 34a, 35b, 36a; *Talmud Yerushalmi, Sotah* 7:5.

2. Commentaries on Gemara:

Rashi; Maharal; Maharsha; Maharatz Chayos; Korban HaEidah; Pnei Moshe.

3. Midrash:

Bereishis Rabbah 49:2, 76:4; *Yalkut Shimoni, Yehoshua* 8.

4. Commentaries on Midrash:

Yefei To'ar; Eitz Yosef; Chiddushei HaReshash.

Sources   201

5. Commentaries on Tanach:
   Rashbam; Even Ezra; Akeidas Yitzchak; Ramban; Rashi; Radak; Ralbag; Abarbanel; Alshich; Da'as Mikra; Metzudas David; Yalkut Me'am Lo'ez; Malbim; HaKsav V'Hakabbalah; Or HaChaim; Torah Temimah; Rav Yaakov Fidanque.

6. Explanations on Tanach:
   Rav Mordechai Miller.

Chapter 8: David Vanquishes Golias

1. Gemara:
   Sotah 42b.

2. Commentaries on Gemara:
   Rashi; Maharal.

3. Midrash:
   Vayikra Rabbah 17:3, 21:2, 26:8; *Midrash Tanchuma HaYashan* (Buber), *Vayigash* 8; *Yalkut Shimoni, Shmuel* I, 17.

4. Commentaries on Midrash:
   Yefei To'ar; Matnos Kehunah; Eitz Yosef; Maharzav.

5. Commentaries on Tanach:
   Targum Yonasan; Rashi; Ralbag; Radak; Abarbanel; Rabbeinu Yeshayah; Malbim; Chidda; Tzenah U'Renah; Metzudas David; Da'as Mikra.

6. Explanations on Tanach:
   Rav Chaim Shmulevitz; Rav Mordechai Miller.

Chapter 9: The Altar

1. Mishnah:
   Middos 1:6, 3:4.

2. Commentary on Mishnah:
   Rav Pinchas Kehati.

3. Gemara:
   Tosefta, Bava Kamma 7; Zevachim 54a; Sukkah 48b, 49a.

4. Commentary on Gemara:
   Rashi.

5. Midrash:
   Mechilta 11: 7–8; *Midrash Tanchuma, Yisro* 17; *Midrash Lekach Tov, Yisro* 23.

6. Commentary on Midrash:
   Eitz Yosef.

7. Commentaries on Tanach:
   Seforno; Rashbam; Rashi; Ramban; Even Ezra; Akeidas Yitzchak; Gur Aryeh; Kli Yakar; Torah Sheleimah; Da'as Mikra; Torah Temimah; Yalkut Me'am Lo'ez; Rav S. R. Hirsch.

Chapter 10: The Temple

1. Mishnah:
   Pirkei Avos 5:8

2. Commentaries on Mishnah:
   Midrash Shmuel; Tosafos Yom Tov.

3. Gemara:
   Tamid 26b; *Sotah* 48b; *Gittin* 68a.

Sources

4. Commentaries on Gemara:
   Rashi; Maharal.

5. Midrash:
   Shir Hashirim Rabbah 1:5; *Koheles Rabbah* 1:1; *Pesikta Rabbasi* 6.

6. Commentaries on Midrash:
   Eitz Yosef; Yedei Moshe; Maharzav; Radal; Chiddushei HaRashash.

7. Commentaries on Tanach:
   Ramban (Shemos 20:22); *Radak; Metzudas David; Da'as Mikra; Malbim.*

$\dfrac{80''}{68}$ Ἐόρτα